# WISDOM IN THE MIRROR

By Pastor Keith Chilson

# TABLE OF CONTENTS

# DEDICATION

This book is dedicated to the Lady who has helped me find family, in every way possible, my wife of 47 years, MaeVaughan Chilson. Without her patience, faithfulness, love, forgiveness, and so much more, I could never have found the joy of family that I have so longed for, and that I now possess.

Thank you to my four children, Krystal Garces, Shari Marshall, Ryan Chilson, and Kara Armstrong for the incredible joy and pride you have each brought into my life.

# INTRODUCTION

Growing up without affection, and missing the "family" ingredient in our family situation as a child, has left me with a deep desire to be "family" with my family. That desire has given me the motivation to leave behind something for each successive generation of my descendants. Something of who I am, and of the Lord Jesus' presence and working in my life. For that reason I have written this book. This book is not written for the general public, though, they are welcome to read it. It is written very specifically with my direct descendants in mind, that is my children, grandchildren, great grandchildren, and continuing. You are my target audience.

The stories included in this book are a selection that span most of my life, and have been chosen for both the story itself, and the applied lesson that each story offers. It is my hope that those who read this book, especially my descendants, will enjoy the stories and benefit from the brief lessons that I apply at the end of each story. It is my hope that this book will be kept by my descendants, and passed down from generation to generation becoming somewhat of a "family tie" throughout the generations. I also hope that this book will be an inspiration to those who read it, stirring in some of them the desire to do the same, and in so doing, to add to the history or our lineage.

May this book add to the sense of "family" in my family for generations to come. Each person in this family is unique and will experience their own stories in their time and place. May what I have written here help each of you with your stories as they occur, giving them meaning and perhaps saving the reader some embarrassment, struggle, or pain, in the process.

I love you all! Those I know and those of you whom I will never know in this world. Because you are in me, you dwell in my love and I live just a little bit through your lives, influencing your stories with mine, creating one big and wonderful story through us all.

# CHAPTER 1
## I QUIT - THE FIRST TIME

It had been a bad Sunday morning. I was just 17 years old and the conviction of the Holy Spirit had worked overtime on me for things done during the week at school. I had not given in to the Spirit, thinking that I just couldn't seem to change some things and that it was time for me to quit. The pastor had ended the service early saying that the Spirit was dealing with someone and that He (the Spirit) had told the pastor not to proceed until that person yielded to the promptings of the Spirit. I had spent a miserable afternoon. The Sunday night service was a repeat of Sunday morning. To make matters worse, the pastor was my foster dad. I found myself standing outside of a church window listening in the dark, as the pastor prayed, worshipped, and wept before the Lord. What he was going through was my fault. I decided that the least I could do was tell him that I was the problem and let him off the hook. As I stood in the back of the small sanctuary waiting, the pastor soon looked up and asked what I wanted. I told him that it was me. I was the one the Spirit of God was trying to reach. And before I could give my explanation, he said, "Then you're the one who should be here, not me." He set his guitar down and left through the back door.

Feeling suddenly very isolated and on the spot, I walked slowly to the wooden altar bench at the front, paused for a moment, and then knelt before the Lord for what I thought would be the last time. I briefly expressed to Jesus how I just couldn't seem to do what He wanted and rather than continue to weary and embarrass Him, I quit.

As I placed the palms of both hands on the altar bench and attempted to rise it was then that I was suddenly aware of what felt like a large hand covering my entire back and not allowing me to rise. I pushed harder saying, "I'm sorry, I quit." No matter how much I struggled to rise, it was just impossible for me to get off my knees. I do not know just how long this conflict waged, but it seemed like a very long time to me as I struggled physically and emotionally with the weight that held me on my knees.

Finally, with a feeling of exhaustion and defeat, I whispered, "Okay, I'll try just one more time." The response of God was a clear, "That is all I've ever asked."

What had become an accumulation of failures to me was apparently just one more good start for the Lord. I did not know of the verse that says "grace upon grace" at that time. I just knew that He forgave me much easier than I forgave myself, again and again and again.

Long before I failed, He had given an unbeatable solution. No matter how I failed or how many times I failed He had already covered it. I just needed to receive it.

It would be years before I could arrange that event in scriptural terms, but its power in my life has grown with every failure. Through the years as I have pastored churches and ministered to God's kids, I have come across a fair number of them who were where I was at that altar. I quit! They were not people who wanted to go back to the world; they were people who did not want to disappoint their Savior - again. The repeated sin is agony often because we see what it cost the Lord Jesus. Quitting, however, is not the path to take.

I don't know how many times I have made a fresh start. I do know that it has been more often than I can count. I don't know why God is so patient and full of grace; I just know that He is. I have not to date found a limit line with God on this one and for that I rejoice! In all of this, God has never lowered His standards nor has He withdrawn His commands upon my life. He never reduces Himself; He just increases us. He places us in the position for a fresh start with no strings attached each time.

So if you find yourself at the end because of things you have done, just remember, your end of the line is God's starting block with all weights removed. Fresh and full of hope and glory. I pray that you will find yourself unable to quit no matter how many times you have fallen. I suspect that He believes in you more than you believe in yourself, or Him, for that matter. Not because you can do it. No-no-no! But because He can do all things, even in and with you.

# CHAPTER 2
## A LEAP OF FAITH

I really looked up to my older brother growing up.  His three-plus years more of life than mine seemed to make him so much wiser and smarter than me.  It was a bit of a myth in reality, but that was what I thought at the time.  So when he suggested something new, well, he was older and he would know what I did not.  So when he suggested that we could parachute off of the cliff behind our house, I was easily convinced.

According to him, all we needed was the top sheets off of our single beds and a running start.  I was all in.  Drifting lazily down to the sand some 20 to 30 feet below sounded like a marvelous adventure.  And, of course, we couldn't tell mom because the sheets might get dirty and she would object.  Yep!  I bought that too.  So we made off with the sheets and went to the top of the sandstone bluff where I received my instructions, going first, of course.  After all, I was younger and lighter.

Just hold two corners of the sheet in each hand, drape the sheet over your back, run, and jump, snapping the sheet up over your head and enjoy the ride.  Man, am I glad there was sand down there and not rocks or brush or something else. My lazy drift turned out to be a screaming meteoric plummet, and my landing was worse.  My brother was quickly at my side, having climbed down and not using his parachute for some reason. He was brushing sand, away asking if I was all right and saying, "Don't tell Mom!" What?  Is he still worried about a couple of sheets?  Of course not, but it would be a few years before I would catch on.

Over the years as an adult, I've received advice that has reminded me of that event so long ago.  It's kind of funny how free people can be with advice that doesn't affect them.  Just have faith!  Only believe!  Go ahead, you'll see, it will be great!  Trust me!  Sounds like a bed sheet to me.  Faith is not something to throw down like a tarp over a mud hole.  It is not a self-constructed bridge over the river of want. And most certainly faith is not proof of His presence, but rather His presence is proof of faith. We don't prove our faith; He, in response to our faith, proves Himself - to be faithful.

The next time an older brother suggests you take a bed sheet and jump off a cliff, tell Mom first! The older brother may be interested in the upcoming event, but Mom is concerned about you, and those two things are different. Of course, Mom here represents the wisdom of a mentor / pastor with relationship and experience. Don't get drawn into the excitement of doing something on a leap of faith that really calls for the grounding of wisdom and knowledge. Your landing may not be as sandy as mine was. You might not survive and it may be too late for Mom to help much. We can easily be deceived by things we know too little about. The influence of others that calls for a leap of faith may be in reality a test of your faith. I have seen the aftermath of some of those leaps of faith. Destruction beyond belief.

There are so many things that I have found this little episode in my life to have helped me with. From foolish attempts to prove God through ridiculous demonstrations of behavior, to subversive doctrines that end in pain and sorrow rather than joy and peace. The scripture tells us to "know those who labor among you." We are reminded to listen to them and honor them. Getting wise counsel is never an act of unbelief. So leap if you will, but be sure to clear it with Mom first!

# CHAPTER 3

## ENDURING ENEMIES

I will call him "John," though that is not his name. He was mean to the point of cruelty. He seemed to live just to make my life miserable. I disliked him thoroughly. I was 24 and he was perhaps in his mid 30s. We were working together as part of a team, and he chose me as his daily target for bullying and belittling. He threatened me constantly and sought to incite others to pick fights with me. Because of him, I did not have a single friend there where I worked. These were rough men. It was a North Coast lumber mill, after all, and these would not be counted as the cream of any crop. I just wanted out of this, but the Lord seemed to be denying my pleas for another means to support my family.

My wife and I had gone through a very difficult experience with the birth of our second child during this time, ending up with a mountainous hospital bill, and I needed the money this particular job offered. I hated the work, but I needed the job more than I hated the job, It was this tough time in my life that forced me to stay with this miserable job. So I endured this man that I thought of as an enemy, trying to stay within the bounds of good Christian behavior but not liking any of it at all.

My lunchtimes were mostly spent alone, away from the lunchroom among the piles of lumber by myself day after day, week after week. I did not understand how this was glorifying God, but as far as I could tell it was His will for me for the time. I just endured from clock-in to clock-out and then left as fast as I could.

Then one day as I was walking among the stacks of lumber at lunchtime, I heard a quiet weeping coming from nearby. I slipped over and peaked between the rows of lumber, and there sat my nemesis, bent over with his head in his hands just quietly weeping. After a brief pause and some self-debate, I slipped over to him. He heard me coming and looked up quickly, wiping his eyes and said,

"Oh, it's you." I asked what was wrong and if there was anything I could do to help. After a couple of minutes of silence, John leaned forward again, and with a fresh stream of tears told me that his wife had left him last night, and he didn't know if he could live without her. We talked quietly for a few minutes, and then I prayed with him. John told me he didn't want anybody else to know and I assured him they would not find out from me.

My job changed that day. Things got easier, people were not so hard on me, and John treated me like I was a good friend. I know that others wondered what had happened, but to my knowledge neither John nor I said anything to anybody. I had thought all that time that this job was about the money I had asked for in my prayers. Then I found out it was more about someone else's pain than mine. Funny how God can answer two prayers at the same time.

Sometimes things just are not bad enough yet for God to break in on someone's life. And while He is waiting for things to reach a turning point, He just might need someone who will persistently endure for a season. Don't retaliate. Don't quit. Just wait, not knowing what God has on His mind until the time is right and the pain is enough to open a heart to the Healer. I wish I could say that John got saved that day, but I can't. What I do know is that he found out on that day that I was different than all of the rest, and that Jesus loves him. I suspect that the experience tenderized something in him, and I like to think that just maybe, when the time was right, that seed sprouted and John found the One who would never leave him. The Bible says that Moses endured the shame, and that Jesus endured the cross. The Apostle Paul endured years of prison for the sake of witnessing to the household of Caesar, and John endured a lengthy exile. Paul instructed Timothy to endure hardship as a good soldier. Enduring hardship and enemies is not high on the list of ways we want to glorify our Lord, but I suspect it is a job with few applicants and lots of room for newcomers. Popularity is big on Christian bucket lists these days. But somehow I really doubt that God needs a lot of popular people. Enduring is hard, but it can bear fruit in soil where nothing else will work. The next time you come up with a tough setting, try to endure as a good soldier. You just might be the answer to another's pain and prayer, while God is answering your own pain and prayer at the same time.

# CHAPTER 4

## PAIN BITES

When I was about 8 years old, I had adopted a mongrel puppy. He was full of life and my best friend. We did everything together. He followed me down a country road one day as I headed to the old country store for some penny (actually two for a penny) candy. En route, as he investigated everything along the way, he was run over by a pickup. He was still alive but not doing well. The driver stopped, said he was sorry, then loaded my puppy and myself up and took us home. As I knelt later that day by the pillow my puppy was laying on listening to him whimper (I was only wearing a pair of worn out jeans) he lashed out and bit me on my bare foot. I stood up in shock. My mom, having seen this, came over and knelt beside me as tears formed in my eyes. Then she said something that I have never forgotten and have relied upon for almost 60 years. Her words, "Honey, your puppy didn't bite you, his pain did. Don't blame him for what his pain does."

It is amazing what our pain will cause us to do to one another, even our best friends. I have for almost 60 years now tried to heed her words. I hope that if and when my pain bites someone, they will not blame me for what my pain does. One of the things that set Jesus apart from everyone else is the fact that He restrained His pain, never giving it the chance to bite anyone, not even those who drove the nails into his hands and feet. He went to the slaughter silent. He bore our pain and His. I hope that I can one day learn to be more like Him in this matter. Pain may work in us, but it should not work through us. Life is not pain free, but it should be bite free.

On the other hand there are many times when we get bit by another's pain, and the shock of that bite often wounds us in the depth of our soul. When this happens, if the wound is not properly tended, it will become a source of resident pain that will suddenly and unexpectedly lash out at others around us for a long time to come. When this happens, our pain can set off a chain reaction of bites and pain that can span generations and spread to multiple families. I have sat with people who were full of pain that began in someone else a long time ago. The original wounded person now long gone but the pain of their wound still wreaking havoc on lives years and generations later.

Letting go of pain is an important skill in this life. If we do not release it, it will fester in us. A bite from another that has become a resident pain in yet another will fester because we blame others who bite out of their pain. Yes, pain often bites, but love for the one in pain will cut the chain of bites off at its origin. Don't blame folks for what their pain does. You may need to keep a little distance to be safe. Find a way if you can to help relieve their pain, and tend your wound carefully if you receive one. It will set you both free and prevent a long chain reaction of bites and pain. Life isn't pain free, but with some work, the pain can be removed, and love can flow with liberty, relieving us of the nasty reaction of biting out of pain, especially with those we care about. Going barefoot around friends shouldn't be dangerous.

# CHAPTER 5

## TOUGH DECISIONS - TOUGHER TRIALS

My wife and I were sitting in a doctor's office. She was in the early stage of her second pregnancy, and she had been exposed to a disease that in the majority of cases resulted in deformity and retardation in the newborn infant if carried to full term. The doctor was advising us against keeping this child. He said that abortion was a "safe alternative." Safe for whom? I wondered. There was only one answer to this: keep and love this child as a gift from God no matter what. We did worry some. We prayed much. We didn't say much to people.

When our second daughter was born, she was not deformed in any fashion, but because of a congestion in her sinuses, she was unable to breathe through her nose. And being an infant, she did not know how to breathe through her mouth, so she cried non-stop. After a couple of days, the doctors told us that there wasn't anything they could do but watch her and that we stood a good chance of losing her due to this. They also said that we could watch her, at home if we wanted to. We agreed, took our crying infant and went home.

I went to work the next day and my wife sat at home with a blood clot due to the delivery, trying in vain to comfort our baby. The weakness that she was showing as she labored to breathe without rest or the ability to eat was excruciatingly painful. That evening after I came home and took over the duty of vain comfort, my wife, having endured all she could, went to bed not expecting her baby to be alive in the morning. After several hours of pleading before the Lord I could take no more. I laid her on the couch and prayed, "She is yours, I release her to you," and then I turned and walked away. Within three steps there was silence, and I stopped with my head down, not wanting to go back to what I would find but knew I had to deal with this too. When I picked her up, she was asleep, breathing normally, and I began to cry.

To this day, my wife and I still don't honestly know what that was all about. We rejoice in the great mercy of our Lord, but we remain mostly ignorant as to what was going on in the heavenlies during this time. I can tell you this, trusting God to take her was a lot harder than trusting God to keep her. Sometimes the right decision is the hardest one, and it promises a life of trials. We must learn not to make decisions to ease our burden but rather to make decisions that allow us to bear the burden of the Lord. There are many times when we are faced with a decision that if made correctly will result in an added burden in life. However, if made incorrectly, it could result in an unbearable burden for eternity. Decisions can be tough, and the consequences even tougher, but doing the wrong thing for the sake of ease or comfort is not a compromise that should be made.

# CHAPTER 6

## SAFE IN THE STORM

Our friend's dog, a Collie much like the original Lassie, had given birth to a litter of puppies whose father was a very large German Shepherd. We were invited over to take our pick of the litter, of which there were several. As we looked over the bunch of as yet-too-small-to-take-home possibilities, they were all squirming and wriggling as they competed for the dinner table. One, in particular, caught our attention as, unlike the rest, he was not whimpering but was growling fiercely and pushing all contestants to the side. Someone commented that he was a tough little guy, and he was named right there on the spot "Tuffy" and designated the newest member of our family.

At 12 years of age, I was in love with this fierce furball from first sight of him, and in due time, Tuffy and I became inseparable. We lived in a rural farming area, and the laborer's house that we lived in was in the middle of what seemed to me to be fields without end. My four-legged and quite-furry companion and I would wander for hours and for miles as we forged new adventures every day. We dug up mice and ground squirrels, we chased rabbits and birds, and we investigated every corner of our wide-open world. He soon grew to weigh over 100 pounds and became my personal bodyguard.

On one occasion as we were crossing a field occupied by a bunch of range cattle on our way home from investigating a seagull's nesting area, one of the new moms of the range took exception to my presence and with head down charged me. I took off as fast as I could in a sprint but was fearfully aware that I was going to lose this race. As I looked back over my shoulder to judge the timing of this collision, I saw Tuffy running even alongside of the mad mother, and I slowed as my four-legged bodyguard leapt to sink his teeth into the nose of this threat to my well-being. As I stopped and turned to watch the outcome of the clash, I watched the range renegade, with dog firmly attached to her nose, do a complete end-over-end flip landing with a ground jarring thud and a large cloud of dust. As the dust cleared, I could see the two combatants standing stock still, nose to nose with less than six inches separating them. They stood that way for some time with Tuffy emitting a menacing growl any time the cow attempted to move. Eventually Tuffy looked my way, back at the cow, and then trotted over to stand by me. We strolled calmly and unbothered to the fence where, after crawling through, we continued home as if nothing had happened. Just another day of adventure.

I had no idea that my canine companion could or would defend me against a critter that weighed about eight times what he weighed. So there in some rancher's field, where I probably should not have been doing things that did not need to be done, I found out that I was fairly safe from threats that I could do nothing about myself. That episode changed my attitude for every adventure thereafter with Tuffy. I was confident in my safety and even wished to have another episode just to watch the deliverance show. Nothing had changed about me, other than I was now equipped with the knowledge of something that had been with me all along, howbeit unknown to me.

Through the years as life has attacked me like a mad mother cow, I have found the same sense of safety in the companionship of Jesus through the presence of the Holy Spirit. On more than one occasion, as a threat that was considerably beyond my ability to handle or escape has loomed, I have watched as my heavenly bodyguard would, often at the last minute, throw the threat for a loop and then escort me on my way.

I have found that many of God's kids are unaware of the Comforter that abides with us as kind of a spiritual nanny watching over the offspring of the Lord. Jesus said, "I will not leave you without a Comforter who is just like Me." This just may be the greatest promise to the New Covenant child of God; the presence of God via the Holy Spirit. No other promise relating to this life can compare to this one. He, the Spirit of God, has defended me in earthly matters great and small. His presence is my confidence. His presence is the greatest proof of my sonship to the Father. The Scriptures tell us that without the Spirit's presence, we are none of His. He is God's seal of sonship, and He is my Divine Bodyguard. It is not up to me to do it right, though I need to learn to do just that, It is rather up to the Spirit of the Presence of God to lead me right, and on that He never fails.

So when you find yourself in a sprint with danger on your heels, if you look closely, you will see the Spirit of the Lord standing with and for you. He watches over you with a passionate jealousy that is unmatched anywhere. So dare to trust Him, for He has been given charge over your well-being.

# CHAPTER 7

## HE GOES AHEAD

We knew that our time was nearing an end in the church we were currently pastoring. We had not said anything to anyone. Then one morning as I was praying, I distinctly heard the Spirit say that we would be moving to a specific rural town where one of my mentors lived and was pastoring. He had been pastoring there for a number of years and was still relatively young, in his late 40s, and I knew it was his intention to remain there until retirement. Yet I was certain that the Lord was saying that I would be moving there and assuming the pastoral role. This did not make any sense, but it was so clear to me.

As I wrestled with this, I sensed the Lord telling me that I needed to call a man that was a mutual friend of both of us and tell him what the Lord had told me, without contacting the pastor in the town where we were to go. Again, it made no sense, but it was so clear and strong. So I complied. After speaking with this third party, he had nothing particular to say and seemed to be unsure of why I was calling him. I had done what I felt was asked of me, so I just dropped it. About a week later, the third-party friend called me and shared a strange story. It seems as though the mentor/pastor of the rural town that I believed God was directing me toward had called him also and shared his own situation. He had found himself in divorce proceedings, and as he was praying on what to do, the Lord had told him to call our third-party friend and tell him that the Lord had said that I needed to come and pastor the church, even though no one else even knew he would be resigning. So now there were three witnesses to this odd sense of direction.

The urge in the Spirit was so strong that I resigned from my church, packed up my family, and moved to this town without even communicating with the church I intended to pastor, other than with a friend there and his wife who helped us move. We just moved to town and started attending the church where our mentor pastored, as they went through the turmoil of the pastor's divorce and resigning. It would be another two months before I would be considered for the role of pastor. When the time came, the vote was 100% in favor of me assuming the pastorate. I knew that I would be pastoring that church before that church knew they would need a pastor. God was way out ahead of all of us, bringing together the pieces and preparing us with His plan for us.

When we live by the revealed will of God, we find that He is always way out ahead of us, arranging the pieces, dealing with the necessary people, and solidifying His plan. Virtually every move I have ever made from the time that I was saved was done in this fashion. I have known for as much as two years ahead of time where I would be, even though there was no evidence of an opportunity or a need. I knew of my retirement and how it would happen twenty five years before it happened. Though no move was involved, it happened just as the Lord had said it would. But that is another story.

The future is not to be feared by those who know the One who is already there and waiting for us. Knowing ahead of time does not make it easy: it does give a sense of confidence, though, even when the evidence is still missing. I believe that Jesus spoke to this in an indirect fashion when He said that He was going (to heaven) to prepare a place for us. If our place in heaven has been made ready two thousand years before we were scheduled to show up, I feel quite confident that my places of residence here have been prepared for me way in advance as well.

Change and obedience can be difficult, especially when it involves everything we own and all that we know. All that we do in obedience to Him now as Christians is but an extension of His own obedience in surrendering to Calvary. His obedience made the way for ours.

He knew about Calvary long before the participants showed up. I suspect He knew each name and each story of all of those who

24

were there as He kept His date with our destiny.  Yes, the Cross of Christ in some fashion is our destiny.  Judgement.  Pain. Embarrassment. Rejection. Suffering.  And don't forget the death part.  All of that in some divine and mysterious way set a path for each one who would yield to Him as Lord and surrender both their past and their future to the one who has the title deed on both.

You will never end up in a place that the Lord of Glory does not own and has not already arranged in expectation of your arrival. Our past was dealt with in His death, our future belongs to Him through His resurrection, the ever-present now being His by right of the throne He occupies at the right hand of the Father.  So fear not! Let change come.  You will always find He was there way ahead of you and has your place in tomorrow all prepared.

# CHAPTER 8

## AN INCOGNITO ANGEL

As I sat in my office working on the midweek Bible study, I was feeling a little pressed as I had an appointment in town in a short time and too much to do here to finish before I went to my appointment. My office was downstairs half of a flight and close enough to the front door of the small church I pastored that I could hear the church door open and close with my office door open. The location of the church on a highway in a rural setting meant that I often had visitors that were somewhat suspect in their appearance and lifestyle, and I did not want unnoticed visitors wandering around in the building.

As I was bent over a pad of paper (yep, using a pen not a computer) with my eyes focused on my work, I had that eerie sense that I was being watched. So I lifted my eyes just slightly and sure enough, there, standing in my doorway, was a fellow with dark blond hair, a very faded flannel shirt and jeans, and I had not heard him come in which made me quite suspicious and a little edgy. He was, by my estimation, just over six feet tall, slender of build, and had the lightest blue eyes I had ever seen. His words to me as I noticed him were something like, I am sorry to interrupt you, but I have a little free time and when that happens I like to drop into a church and play a piano. I am between assignments (that did not register at the time) and have some time and was wondering if I could play one of your pianos?

I suggested that he have a seat and maybe we could talk a little first. I was thinking that this was something I did not need now and yet did not want to be discourteous, and still I needed to determine if I could grant his request. As we talked briefly I asked a couple of questions that I remember, the first being, "Tell me about yourself. What do you do?" His response was very vague and a little criptive, "I do all kinds of things. I take assignments and seldom have time between them. I have some time now. That is why I

26

would like to play a piano." So I tried again, "Tell me something about your family and what they do." Again the answer was vague, "I'm from a very large family and (here he paused briefly to consider his answer) I think you would call them farmers." Not sensing anything threatening, I grabbed a couple of booklets I used for witnessing, led him into the fellowship hall just around the corner and to a very old and out-of-tune piano where I told him, "These booklets are for you when you leave, and I have an appointment in 30 minutes so at that time you will need to leave." I watched as he used his right index finger to strike a key causing me to think, "Oh, brother, he doesn't really know how to play a piano."

I returned to my office, keeping the door open to listen for anything out of place, and went back to work. Quickly I heard the sound of piano music unlike anything I have heard before, beautiful, and with a sense of flooding the downstairs of the building. I was somewhat awestruck by it. I returned to my study for what seemed like just a minute and looking up he was standing in front of my desk with the booklets I had left for him. He very gently set the booklets down on my desk, patting them with a sense of affection and then said, "It is time for your appointment. You have given me a gift. I want to leave something with you." that being said, he went on to say, "Amos 3:7 - The Lord God will not do anything in the earth without first telling His prophets."

I was standing just two steps from him as he quickly turned toward the door and started running. For reasons I cannot explain, I ran after him, following him out the office door seeing him clear three steps at a time, taking two strides up the stairs, with me trying to catch up, and then -- he just -- disappeared. I ran to the front door and threw it open to see -- nothing. I ran down the walk and nothing. I ran back into the building and upstairs to the sanctuary and nothing. I walked slowly back downstairs to my office and sat down to try to grasp what had just happened. Then I went to my appointment with a head full of chaotic questions and no idea what I had just witnessed or why.

I was so intent on chasing this guy that the book, chapter, and verse he quoted were lost to my memory, and I had no idea what he meant, not realizing at the time that he was quoting that particular verse from Amos. I remembered and pondered what he had said, minus the chapter and verse, off and on for years, having come to the conclusion that this had been an angel, and I had missed the opportunity of a lifetime. I could not believe the foolish questions I had asked, and I could think of thousands I wanted to ask, but it was much too late for that now. Why tell me that? Was I supposed to do something? Was something about to happen? Did this really happen?

It was a few years later, just a few months before I retired from pastoring that I received a text from my daughter who was reading in her devotions from the book of Amos chapter 3 and verse 6, asking me what that meant. I opened my Bible, read that verse and then backed up to verse 1 to read the whole context, coming to a mind-numbing stop on verse 7, "Surely the Lord God will do nothing, but he revealeth his secret unto his servants the prophets." My mind and my heart began to race, and my daughter's question faded as I remembered my encounter with this verse on the lips of a heavenly messenger. Here I was brought back to what I had missed, with clarity. God was speaking and something was about to happen, the beginning of a change. The change itself and the things that have occurred since are material for a later episode.

I have said all of that to say this. It is the way of men to live their lives as if it is common day-to-day stuff. We are not in any way looking at our days as events in the divine and eternal timeline with potential for holy moments of interaction that go beyond our daily expectations. We are, because of this, prone to missing some incredible and awe -inspiring moments, perhaps even days, as a result of how we live. We live outside of the sense of expectation that something will happen today, and as a result we bypass all kinds of encounters, most of these with family and friends many with coworkers and acquaintances. And as the Scripture says, a few with visitors, strangers who are not of this world. I now wonder how many chances to share affection, encouragement, and kindness do we pass up because in our minds our day is already planned? What difference could we have made but didn't because we felt busy? What relationships we bypassed because we were suspicious or edgy or just self-centered? And what miracles did we miss out on because we were keeping a schedule instead of seeing what sat right in front of us?

It seems to me that there may just be more in the intent of our Creator in how and why we live than we allow for. I can now look at crowds of people and wonder if there are any visitors from above in the group? What gifts are there that are walking around unnoticed? What problems or pain am I looking at and not seeing? How can I change how I live to become more engaged in what the Lord may be trying to do right here in front of me? All of this is something that I am still trying to figure out, but at least now I know that there is far more to what I am seeing and hearing than I am prone to consider.

Perhaps we can train ourselves to see what and who is present with us with a bit more clarity and patience than we would normally possess. It is worth a try considering what just may be missed if we don't try. Not only encounters of the heavenly kind but interaction with one another of a deeper and more meaningful nature. Like taking advantage of an unscheduled opportunity to enlarge an already important relationship with understanding and affection. Who knows? This all might just be something that is being recorded somewhere important for future reference. Maybe we should look more if we want to see more. Just maybe.

# CHAPTER 9

## A FATHER'S ADVICE

As our eldest child graduated from high school and turned 18, I made one of the tougher decisions in my life, one that would guide my relationships with my children when they came of age. I decided that I would not offer personal advice to them unless there was some indicator from them that told me they were looking for it. I was keenly aware of the risks of this policy of "I'll ride along while you drive" approach to life with my of-age offspring. I fought some intense battles with myself as I watched each of them approach a fork in the road, and I spent some anxious hours praying while they steered their own lives. I did not tell them that I would behave in this manner, I just did it and complained to my wife when I was afraid for their failures. I am not recommending this approach. It is somewhat personal and I was watching the results of 18 years with each one to see what had taken root and what had been uprooted.

One of my goals was to create a bond where they felt free to approach me as my adult child without having to fight for their own validity or identity. These had already been given them, though they were yet to be found by each. I wanted them to have their own validation before they honestly knew what it was. They were not establishing something; they were discovering it. They all made some mistakes, some rather serious, but they all seemed to end up flying by the basic guidelines that they grew up with. I felt like I needed to trust them with life if they were going to trust me with pieces of it as they encountered it.

Eventually they each began to understand that if they wanted Dad's counsel, they would have to ask for it. The amazing thing is that the older they get, the more they seem to seek it out. I have never had to climb over the wall of their defenses to speak to things that could bring pain and loss. We seem to have developed a common quiet trust that I enjoy, and I hope that is meaningful to them.

I view my relationship with Father God in a similar fashion. He quietly waits nearby as I discover my need for His assistance in life. I am often slow to seek His advice, and He is at peace with my struggle in my true identity as His son. Like a child, I often attempt to do by myself what is better done with His help. His patience is boundless, and I see in Him the example that I want to emulate with my daughters and son. I don't see my Heavenly Father as fighting for a place in my life, but rather as One who knows He has a place and waits for me to engage with it. Coming from a broken and dysfunctional earthly home I see in Father God the example I long to duplicate and pass on. He is always ready with wisdom and information when I need it, yet leaving ample room for me to discover what He has always known. His joy in my discovery of life is mirrored by my own joy as my children discover life. What a marvelous view when the past is anchored in the future and the future is unfolded from the past. That is to say, looking up at my Heavenly Father as I find my likeness to Him and seeing it emerge in my own offspring. I pray that each of my own children find the discovery of enjoying their children's discovery of life as much as I have with them. The quiet unnoticed smiles of a parent who sees what the child misses in the midst of things and the contentment experienced as they discover what you have known for a very long time are rewards enough for a word well spoken.

Giving a word of advice is a tremendous responsibility, especially for a parent. The circumstances of a parent's past that lead to advice about a child's future makes that word of advice a bridge over which generations cross. My advice passed on could become a family way or tradition. What is a moment of wisdom to me could be a heritage to the family. Words of advice spoken in haste or fear could become a bondage for future generations. Giving advice should always be done with great care. It just might become the next prison for someone you love or it could be the safety net that preserves multiple generations. I pray that I listen well to Father God so I have good stuff to pass on to kids that I leave behind.

Advice is not control. Control is not advice. Advice should breed liberty that is bound by safety. Advice is needed but at times not heeded. Our Heavenly Father knows this all too well, and yet He never withdraws His love or care because we do not hear or accept what He says. May each of us be as committed to those we give wisdom to, even when they toss it aside. May our love exceed our fear. And may our families extend good life from generation to generation until Jesus comes!

# CHAPTER 10

## DISTORTED LENSES

As a young boy I found snakes to be fascinating. I sought them out as companions of sorts. I would find one and then push him down into my pocket and go about whatever other adventures I could find. I would take him out from time to time to make sure he was still with me and then back in my pocket he would go. Sometimes I would have more than one in my pockets by the end of the day. Most of the time I would release them as I headed home but once in a while I would forget and leave my reptilian cargo in the hold of my jeans and that would always become a problem later.

On occasion I would discover on the morrow the now deceased companion and with regret bury him and then start looking for a replacement. On rare occasions, I would leave my slithery friend in a pair of jeans that went into the laundry. Mom, knowing somewhat about little boys, would always check my pockets before throwing my dirty jeans into the wash, looking for rocks and whatnot. On those occasions when she would reach into one of my pockets to discover a serpent, well, she would tend to lose it. She would always yell, and, yes, I mean yell, well, scream to be exact. Then she would give me a lecture about how I was someday going to find a venomous species and then I would be sorry. This lecture was always a prelude to an old-fashioned form of discipline known affectionately as spanking. I always doubted that she was worried about the venomous species so much as the fact that she did not like the "surprise" species that she found in my pants pockets. She thought about snakes differently than I did which brings me to the point behind this story.

I began to understand at a fairly young age that people view things differently. Any number of people might find a snake in a boy's pocket and both the tone with which they speak of it and the words they use to describe it can be multiple, in their expressions, as well as their affections or lack thereof. Some who read this are smiling right about now.  Others are a bit aghast.  There are those who will take on tones of seriousness and those who find all of this very humorous.  This difference I call a "lens", a personal lens, to be more precise.  Nothing changes in the situation.  The only difference is that inner something that causes us to relate to something from our own personal set of values and visions, experiences and fears, and presto!  One story is now multiple in its impacts.  And in its retelling.  Some will speak with tones of fear and disgust, attempting to influence their listeners with their lens as much or more than with the story itself.  Some call this a "bias."  The thing that one speaks of with affection can be spoken of by another with disdain.  And this inner difference is what causes the vast majority of division, strife, pain, sorrow, and so on among people.

Jesus was cruelly crucified for us.  Some weep.  Some mock.  Some rejoice.  The reaction is determined by that inner personal lens or bias that we hold.  That point in our lens where how we will eventually respond finds its origination or focus in what we refer to as the heart.  Not the literal physical heart, but that heart that speaks of our deepest self.  It is our fountainhead of values that is constantly being shaped by experience, relationships, desires and fresh understandings.  It is where we store our pain and sorrow as well as our joy.  It dictates our hopes and controls our expressions.  Jesus said that it was out of this that the mouth will speak.

It is my opinion that few ever really try to stop and look at their lens instead of just looking through it.  We all have these lenses in untold quantity, our favorite food, the entertainment we prefer, the music we like, the personalities we are drawn to, etc.

These lenses also affect our current situations and future.  If we look through the lens of fear we will withdraw or attack.  In this example, fear becomes how what is happening will be recorded in our hearts as well as how this event will shape our future.  If we can change the lens, it is almost as if the event has totally changed.  The impact of the situation on us also changes and how we relate it to others in the future will be altered. All of this change, without a single thing changing in the event that occurs in our life.

Jesus said to His disciples, "You believe in God, believe also in Me." Another way to take that is simply that Jesus is asking us to use Him for our ultimate lens, kind of like saying, "See things through me. Interpret them through me. Respond to them through me. Value them through me." He offers Himself as our personal lens. He does so knowing that while almost nothing that happens will change, its impact and effect in our lives will be radically altered and we will begin to express ourselves in a manner more consistent with His own. Jesus is not just a Savior. He is the source from which we draw and the lens through which we view life, a lens that brings understanding and changes how we think and act, a lens that will refocus every event and relationship for the better.

# CHAPTER 11

## RUNAWAY

According to my memory, I only ran away from home once growing up. I was 13 years old, and I was fed up with nobody caring about me. I didn't seem to matter to anyone in the house, so I took off late one afternoon heading south on Highway 97 from Dorris, California. I didn't grab anything extra as I wanted to travel light and fast to stay ahead of those who would notice my absence and immediately know that I had run away and would, in their sorrow, come desperately searching for me. I will admit to poor planning, as it started to rain about six or seven miles south, and by the time I trotted into Macdoel some ten miles south of Dorris, I was soaked, cold, hungry, and pretty sure that no one was missing me. Only now I was a bit too tired to travel ten miles back home in a cold rain.

After hanging out around the old Macdoel store for a bit, I called a friend of my older brother who lived in Macdoel and who had a car and asked him for a ride back home. Of course, explaining just why I needed a ride was a tad embarrassing. Having secured my transport home, I set to considering just what excuse might be acceptable for my absence of the past few hours. I even prepared my attitude to make sure they would all be sufficiently repentant for their lack of attention to me. I walked in the kitchen door, went through the kitchen which was void of occupants, and through the living room where most everyone sat watching T.V. and then out the front door to give them the chance to pursue me and beg for my forgiveness. I went through the front door out into the dark and stopped. That's when it struck me. No one even knew I had run away. Maybe I really didn't matter. That was one of the loneliest nights of my entire life. Sad, depressed, and miserable I stayed to myself, wondering what was wrong with me. It was a dark night outside but a much darker one in my soul. And there was exactly no one that I could share it with.

I suspect that this is the case with multitudes of people every day and night of every year here on earth, people of all ages and social status. The discovery that you don't matter is worse than almost anything else that can happen to a person. The longing is for far more than acceptance, though that is a big part of what we experience as people. We want purpose connected to a good future. It is fascinating just how strongly we are aimed at the future and how much we need a sense of purpose and expectation in it. We were created with eternity in our souls and with it a longing for a sense of reason beyond our own selves.

Over the years I have encountered a number of surprising cases of people who appeared to be immune to such feelings and need, only to find that they have their own hidden desperate darkness. Many tend to push it down until it no longer will be resisted. It can be a demanding master, searching for light and relationship, both of which have been broken and hidden by the god of this world. The longing is common to humans and it can only be filled within the context of shared companionship and vulnerability, and a sense of hope for the future. And these can only be found in Christ.

This is one of the big reasons why we as God's kids do not respond in kind to those who abuse us verbally or in any way. The darkness hidden within a soul can only be touched by the light of love and kindness that comes through contact with Jesus. There have been countless times when a kind word or deed have pre-empted an attempt at self-destruction or the destruction of another out of hurt and self-misery.

I remember a school bus driver when I was in high school who always called me "sunshine", a misnomer if ever there was one. But I quickly came to look forward (a future word) to the next time I got on the school bus, just to hear that word applied to me. I never once spoke to anyone about how much that meant to me. To speak of it seemed silly, and it made me feel vulnerable to attack, so I kept my feelings hid but revelled in the joy of hearing that one kind word each morning as I climbed on a bus I didn't want to get on to go to a place I didn't like going to. That one word made the rest of the day tolerable.

There are multitudes of people whose day would be changed by a kind word, even from a stranger. That one word might even be a door opener for a budding relationship. It could even be the beginning of a turn from the darkness within to the light of Christ that is the light that is the only thing that can open a portal of love within a life and give people expectations for all eternity.

All men and women need to matter to someone, but especially fulfilling is when we discover that we matter to the One who is the Source of joy and love. And just maybe a person who learns that they do really matter can turn from being a person in need to being a person who meets needs, especially the need to matter with hope for a future that is greater than today.

All relationships have the potential to heal or to wound. A healing relationship is an intentional relationship. It holds the door to tomorrow open until the broken and wounded can manage to crawl through it. It requires great patience with a sense of sight into the distant future that the broken and wounded cannot yet see. Living so that others matter, matters. Oh! The school bus driver? He eventually became my pastor and foster dad and was instrumental in giving me a future. Thanks, Pop! I needed that!

# CHAPTER 12

## FINALLY FREE

It seems to me, though it is probably not accurate, that I was born depressed. I remember feeling sullen and lonely even as a child. I felt that this sense of depression was me, and while I could sometimes mask it before others, I could never escape it. It made me weary inside. I would spend hours as a child off alone seeking out other imaginative worlds that were mostly free from despair. It was the lens through which I viewed everything that went on in my life, a smoky gray distorted lens that never allowed me to find rest or worth.

This monster plagued me years after I met the Lord and well into the years of pastoring. Finally, one day I could take it no longer. I told my wife that I was going away, that I did not know where I was going or when I would return. I am amazed at her understanding and grace in that hour. I packed a few things, climbed into my small pickup truck and just started driving south. If I didn't find an answer, I would return and withdraw from ministry, at the least.

Less than an hour from home I sensed a strong presence of the Lord in my pickup and began to weep as I drove. This was becoming a sort of Gethsemane for me and I needed an intercessor. God the Holy Spirit had volunteered. I don't remember Him saying anything at the time, just that powerful presence that softens and opens for divine access into the closets of our hearts. I can't say that I had any great expectations. It was more a sense of being invaded, painfully yet carefully.

I wound up about seven hours from home at the home of a friend, who lived out in the country. I just knocked and when he answered, I asked if I could stay for a few days and just wander the countryside in prayer. He readily invited me in and extended me a room for as long as I wanted it. Good friends are special treasures. This one has proven to be a very rich treasure.

My friend and his wife would head off to work (he was a rural pastor), and I would walk the mostly traffic-free narrow roads in prayer, punctuated occasionally with false accusations against my God. About midmorning on the third day of this journey, I stopped, looked up toward heaven, and I told the Lord that I could not do it any longer. Either the depression stopped or I was through with ministry. And then He finally broke His silence. He did so with a question as is often His way. He asked me, "Will you stop criticizing My people?" Yes, I was a critic of all of Christendom. I quickly called outloud, "Yes, Lord, I will!" And then something seemed to flood out of my soul. It was like a stagnant pond had been emptied. But it did not stop there. Immediately there was a rush of fresh water refilling my pond. Now, I had been wonderfully filled with the Holy Spirit many years previously. The significant difference with this seemed to be the emptying first. I do not know just how it fits theologically, but I do know that my life changed dramatically at that moment. I wasn't just filled; I had been emptied first. Set free! Long after I had been saved and filled.

My explanation looks something like this. Jesus occupies some rather cluttered and even dirty temples. His occupation today is through the person of His Spirit. But to get a fuller effect from His occupation, sometimes one has to have the temple cleansed, much like in Scripture with the money changers. They were there and so was God in the same temple at the same time. But they were in the way of a fuller ministry by God in His temple. The Scriptures tell us that following the temple cleansing, the children entered to praise and miracles were done there, perhaps for the first time in a long time, and this was years after the Son of God began to attend the temple services in the flesh. I had no idea that I was the problem. I really thought it was God simply not helping me.

It has made me wonder just what kind of clutter is there that prevents the Glory of God from manifesting in our New-Testament Temples. How much more there is that cannot happen without an emptying first? What kind of behaviors or thoughts do we hold to that form stagnant ponds of scum in the Temple of the Most High?

40

I have come to think of the emptying as being as important as the filling.  So when we seek a filling, perhaps we should be open to an emptying first, a cleansing of sorts.  The removal of things that are not in line with Temple purposes.

I have never experienced a moment's depression since that time on that isolated country road where God led me forward with a question.  What I have learned about God and questions is that when He asks one, He is not looking for information but rather is setting the stage to impart inspiration and revelation.  Often a move of God can start with a question from the Throne.  When God asks a question, it is to help you find an answer, not for Him to find one.  Someday I would like to do a thorough study of God questions in the Scriptures.  It might be revealing.  A question from the All-Knowing One just might be your answer in a time of desperation.

# CHAPTER 13

## FUN FOR WHO?

There is at least one other story in this book that speaks of my older brother's influence on my growing up. His name is Jerry. Yes, that is his name, and I mention it here to gain a sort of revenge (I am working on forgiveness still) on him for many of the rather painful experiences that he provided for me as we grew up. He frequently had ideas for things that he said would be "fun", like jumping off a cliff with a bed sheet as a parachute. Or like riding down a long grassy hill - in a metal drum at what seemed to be about the top speed of most locomotives of the time. You know, fun for the guy who puts his little brother in the drum and then gives it a good push to start it down the hill.

He said it would be fun, but like so many other things that I didn't catch on to, he let me go first. It did sound like fun before I crawled into the drum and had second thoughts that he talked me out of. This will be fun! Just brace yourself and it will be fun. And it was fun, just not for me. Jerry seemed to enjoy it a whole lot. What I found out is that a steel drum has no padding and no give when it hits a bump that is magnified by the speed of a locomotive that would give Superman competition. Multiply that by the force and speed of the spinning or rolling drum and you have a lot to scream about. And he never once mentioned that once the ride begins, there are no brakes so no stopping until it is completely over. Fun! I think it was about-half way through this pre-carnival era ride that I decided I did not like fun. Fun for Jerry was painful for me. It was even scary as I was sure it would never end. Later in life I would ponder this fun as I went into open heart surgery. Yeah, fun for whom?

The promise of fun has led many a young person and sometimes an old person into problems that proved to be anything but fun. I have visited people in prison who got there because of fun. I have made hospital calls due to the fun someone said would be there in full measure.  More than one funeral has resulted because of what some well- meaning person said would be fun.

Have you ever noticed how sin always seems to get a hold on us because it seems at first to be fun?  I think that the Bible mentions something about the fun of sin -- for a season.  And what is it about us that we have almost no immunity to that alluring word, fun?  It is also interesting that most people, Christians included, do not sketch a portrait of God as fun.

There are a lot of folks who want to have fun with you, only like my older brother they want you to go first, cause then it will be fun for them.  Beware, little children, of the promise of fun.  You stand a good chance in that setting of being the humor for others at your own expense.  Don't get talked into a drum on a hill without brakes or padding.  Ask yourself, "Fun for whom?" first.  This world is full of folks who have a warped definition of fun.  People who are looking for fun usually are not looking out for the other person.  I love my brother, and I know he had a lot of fun with me growing up.  I just wish I would have had as much fun as he did.

Sometimes people have fun at the cost of another.  Someone's reputation is destroyed because it was fun for -- whom?  A job lost in the name of fun for -- whom?  A marriage broken for the sake of fun for -- whom?  A church split because it was fun for -- whom? Be careful of the fun you agree to.  It just might not end up as fun at all.  Don't get talked into something foolish in the name of fun.  Because by the time you figure out who it is fun for, it might become a bit painful for you for a long time to come.

# CHAPTER 14

## SELF-ESTEEM OR IDENTITY

I was raised by my mom (until the age of 16) and a man that I cared nothing for. I didn't know my earthly dad and at 16 was placed in a foster home with a couple of wonderful people. As a result of this "fatherless" upbringing, I have wrestled with what the counselors called "low self-esteem" for much of my life. I have read books on it and struggled with this and found little help with it until I began to understand the difference between self-esteem and identity.

Much is said today, even in Christian circles about self-esteem. My freedom from not liking myself came as I realized that Jesus died to deliver me from the bondage of self- esteem. The dictionary has literally hundreds of reference to self-hyphenated words, a regular preoccupation with it, in fact. Self-esteem is essentially "belief in one's self" the very thing that Jesus died to free us from. Identity, on the other hand, is the essential quality of being "the same as." Jesus emphasized that He was the "same as the Father" and said that He would send another Comforter who would be "the same as" He. Identity is one of the greatest treasures lost to man when he sinned. When I was born again of the Spirit of God, I became "the same as" Jesus, receiving identity over self-esteem. I am still working at behaving in a manner consistent with my true identity, but I am none-the-less "the same as" He is, and one day when I see Him as He is I will find that I am truly "like Him."

I rejoice in Scripture passages like, "In me that is in my flesh dwells no good thing." Why? Because by the indwelling of His Holy Spirit, I am as like Him as it is humanly possible to be like Him. (We might note here that Jesus gave us what the devil tempted Eve with, just as the Father gave Jesus what the devil tempted Him with.) I have preached and written on the importance of accepting your true Spiritual identity. It is liberating and it enables you to resist the need to fight with everyone around you because you are at peace with who you are, with how you feel about yourself ceasing to be an issue, delivering us from the preoccupation with being offended.

Spiritual identity is one of the great reconciliations that come with salvation. Learning to accept and live in it is difficult for many but when we get it, it takes over and brings liberty to who we are, being the same as He is. The lie in self-esteem is that you need to feel good about yourself. The truth is you need to let who you are in Christ reign over how you feel. Be free, you Children of the Most High, for His identity is imprinted in your spirit and written over your soul, assuring you of a body that one day will mirror His! For as He is so are we by grace through faith.

# CHAPTER 15

## NO ACCOUNTING FOR TASTE

I was pastoring a small rural church, and we were experiencing some growth in the congregation. This seemed to bring out a number of local visitors who wanted to check out what was going on. On one particular Sunday following the service as I stood in the foyer shaking hands and greeting people, a woman who appeared to be in her late 30s with light red hair was exiting the sanctuary. I stuck my hand out and told her that I was glad she had come to service this morning and hoped she enjoyed it. Her response shocked me some. As she shook my hand, she said that she thought that the music and worship were wonderful and that there was a tremendous presence of the Lord, but that in her opinion, I should do the church a favor and resign immediately. I was the only part of the service she objected to, and she objected strongly. I think I mumbled something like, "Oh!" Then she left the building and, to my knowledge she never returned.

Her words were on my mind as I absentmindedly greeted people exiting the sanctuary. It wasn't more than two minutes after the woman with the red hair left when I stuck my hand toward a man I didn't know, greeting him with almost identical words to what I had used with the earlier visitor. His response was to shake my hand with energy and tell me that that was one of the best sermons he had ever heard. He loved how I preached and he would be back. I know that he had not heard the earlier conversation, so I just figured different folks had different tastes.

Since that occasion I have thought quite a bit about those two different responses. What stands out more than the words of each one is the attitude or spirit of each one and how greatly they differed. One's tone was cynical, derisive, and caustic, the other's was full of joy and excitement, demonstrating warmth and gratitude. Attitudes tend to be hard to mask with words. I have come to the place concerning this that I now believe that the difference had little to do with me and really revealed what was happening inside of each of the two listeners in the audience that day. I'm pretty sure that Jesus said something about that occasion long before it happened, back when He said, "Out of the abundance of the heart the mouth speaks."

It should not surprise us when someone opens their mouth and reveals their heart. Their mind is probably working to give credibility to what their heart is spewing, but it never gives validity to the misspoken words, even though the speaker is sure that they have made a good case for it. So this leaves me wondering, just why is it that our mind can be okay with something that is just wrong and living in us, and even go to great lengths to defend the trash that produces such wrong? The only explanation I can come up with is that the heart really does pull the strings in our thinking. Perhaps we should stop once in a while and separate those two, the mind and the heart, so they can evaluate each other. Those two should both come into agreement, but it should be an agreement that includes both the mind and heart of the Lord.

I am sure that you, like me, have heard someone say something a bit out of character with Jesus and then claim to have the "mind of the Lord." There will always be some doubt on that one, because if you don't have His heart as well, you probably are giving credit to the wrong mind. This is a phenomenon that seems to plague many believers, the thinking that having His mind, or in many cases His words, is equivalent to having His heart. It is not so. The mind of Christ will never reveal something that is not already well rooted in His heart. And, likewise, His heart will not release something contrary to the well-being of His mind or words.

Over the years, I've heard a number of Christian leaders issue a call to fight. They say something like, "It's time God's children stood up and fought for what is right!" The way I remember it, Jesus laid down and died for what is wrong. Us! He died for "the sins of the whole world," and He did so while we were still sinning, and, in fact, we were in the act of crucifying the only person to live

47

without sin when He died without objecting to the price for our sin. I seem to recall a passage in one of the Gospels where two of the apostles asked Jesus if He wanted them to call fire down out of heaven to burn up a village in Samaria. They seemed to feel rather safe in this question (do you want?) as they were quoting scripture, emulating a great prophet, defending the Messiah, and opposing some (in their minds) very sinful people who were somehow less deserving of grace than they themselves were. Jesus response was telling. "You don't know that you are of a wrong spirit."

Now, don't get me wrong. I'm all against evil. But destroying people Jesus died for in the name of destroying evil is not likely to rid us of evil, but rather tends to involve us in it to a deeper degree. When we decide to fight, something Jesus forbid His servants to do when He was attacked, we almost always create a devastating mess that it will take Jesus generations to heal. Just read a little church history. In the current age of divine events the best way to defeat evil is with -- good. Love and peace are some of the most formidable weapons (weapons of our warfare) to come out of heaven. The Word of God, our Sword of the Spirit is a love letter, not a nuclear bomb. It is the message of grace and empty graves, not grief and more graves. The hardest two things I have learned to do as a Christian are to 1) wait and 2) respond to evil with love and peace. Yet these have proven to be the most effective weapons I have ever wielded against evil.

So the next time you want to fight, do so by using the opposite weapons of the ones you want to destroy. Be willing to die so that your enemy doesn't have to. Endure hardship like a good soldier of Christ. Let what is in your heart and mind be the same as what is in the heart and mind of the one who died for us all. I am confident that only some will choose this path. But for those who do, the knowledge of the Holy One will be greatly increased. For the others, they will come to an expansive knowledge of war. So what does your taste favor?

# CHAPTER 16

## MILLWRIGHTS AND MECHANICS

A number of years ago I was serving a church (not as pastor) in a rural community in Northern California and working in a small lumber mill. There was a group of older millwrights and mechanics who also worked at this mill -- a crusty bunch at best -- who had lunch together in the shop by themselves. Wanting to witness to them of my faith in Jesus Christ, I walked in uninvited, sat down, and opened my lunch and listened. They were bashing pretty much everything. When they started in on their wives, I had had enough. I began to speak (with five years of marriage) about where they were wrong. One of the bunch, a grizzled and cantankerous old coot, stopped me. Leaning toward me, he said, "Son, in this group you don't have enough history to have an opinion." I was livid, but I shut up and went my way when lunch was over and never went back. My mistake. I thought he was saying that I was not old enough, when he was more likely saying that I was not known enough. Either way I was short on history. I should have had lunch with them every day from then on. I was of the opinion that my opinion, being the right opinion was sufficient. Having the truth is only part of the equation. Having a foundation in relationship with people who need the truth is a key element to reaching this lost world. Making connections with the broken in this world is important to ministry. Often those connections take far more time than we are willing to invest. I have said before that I would trade my sermons to believers to facilitate one more lost sheep in entering the Kingdom. That may not be totally accurate but it does express how I feel about the souls that I have been privileged to lead into the Kingdom.

Paul told Pastor Timothy to "do the work of an evangelist." It wasn't his call or gift, but it was his responsibility. Making a conscious effort to personally reach individuals within our sphere of influence is a responsibility we all carry. So, do the work of an evangelist. It is the biggest need in your community and the greatest investment of time you may ever make.

# CHAPTER 17

## MYSTERIOUS "BUMP BUMPS"

So I'm here, as a techless senior citizen wandering around in this Facebook maze, and I keep running into things I was not looking for. Is that supposed to happen? How does this infernal machine know just what I don't want to do? Then I remembered driving a seven-ton bobtail hay truck at the age of 12 on the road. There was a hole full of springs in the driver's seat, and I had to shove stuff into that to stay in a position to keep hold of the steering wheel. I could reach either the pedals or see through the steering wheel at about a 30-degree angle looking up, but I could not do both at the same time. Then there were these mysterious "bump-bumps." Do all hay trucks do this or just this particular one? A few days later I heard a farmer talk about how some vandal had run over his sprinkler line, taken out a post, and destroyed an irrigation ditch. Vandal? Strong word in my opinion. It was an accident. I didn't mean to do it. And somehow I am not responsible for my accidents. That is when I began to realize that "on accidents" are as costly as "on purposes."

It is that way in relationships as well. Not meaning to hurt or abuse someone still hurts. Life is real and should be lived responsibly. When you feel one of those "bump-bumps" in life, stop and take responsibility. Shoulder the cost because "on accidents" are real relationship breakers. Feelings are not just connected to things done intentionally. The emotional damage itself in many cases lasts a lifetime. Accidents do happen, but they seldom happen without impact or consequences. Expecting an accident victim to just get over it is callous and cruel. Jesus talked about being a good Samaritan when coming across a victim of something done on purpose, but I'm of the mind that victims of accidents fit into that same scenario, especially if the accident is your own. I kinda miss that old hay truck.

51

# CHAPTER 18

## THE MASTER'S IMPROVISATIONAL SKILL

I suppose all of us have been there at one time or another, needing a particular tool that is not available and having to improvise. In place of a hammer, I have used rocks, tree limbs, 2x4s, a screwdriver handle, and even a crescent wrench. I often use my wife's butter knives when I need a screwdriver. I've used a screwdriver as a pry bar and so on. It is my opinion that this is what happens virtually always with God. He has had only one "righteous" tool in all of the history of humanity. He is a genius at improvising. He needs a preacher and uses a plumber. He needs a plumber and uses a preacher. He needs compassion, so he grabs the wounded and works marvelous wonders. I have accomplished a lot with things not meant for the purpose at hand. I have watched God do that very same thing over and over in my life. He doesn't need much more than the chance to get at the problem. I'm not good around people, but He calls me to shepherd them. In my opinion, I'm a poor substitute for a good shepherd, but that has never seemed to bother God. I am poorly educated by today's standards, so he uses me to teach. Don't laugh! You're more of a 2x4 than you are a hammer, yet He uses you to drive home divine points.

Sometimes we are tempted to draw our own sense of "self" worth from the things we have done. That is usually a mistake. It is not so much what we do, as it is the Master's improvisational skill that stands out as a sign or wonder. It has taken me a long time, most of my life in fact, to reach a place where I am more excited about the "hammer problems" God solves with a tree limb than I am about being a tree limb used as a hammer. I suspect even the angels marvel at God's uncanny ability to do things with, in, for and through us to glorify His Name.

He once used a cross as an altar, not to mention a tomb for a nap or a great catch of fish to gain the attention of those followers of His that were in the wrong place doing the wrong thing at the wrong time.  Perhaps that well known verse that says, "I can do all things through Him..." is meant to do more to bring to light His ability than mine. Next time you quote that verse, remember, He is improvising and you couldn't do a thing if He wasn't so good at being -- well -- God!

# CHAPTER 19

## THE POWER OF DIVINE RESTRAINT

The Scriptures speak abundantly about the limitless power of God. It is something that we speak of with liberty and I suspect with a greater amount of ignorance than we are aware of. He still works miracles that astound us, both of the supernatural type such as healings, and those that are hidden in the daily routines of life that are missed by so many. The sun comes up each morning. The power required to fuel the sun boggles our mind, and yet ours is only one of countless stars that burn on the energy of God's holy command. But there is yet another aspect of the omni-ness of God that causes me to want to bow and give praise even now -- again -- as I think about it. It is the immense power of His self-imposed restraint.

The Scripture talks of God "enduring" the vessels fitted for wrath. Restraint! If God has limitless power, than what must the power of His restraint look like? When Jesus was betrayed and arrested, He restrained Himself from acting in the righteousness that would have ended all this evil directed toward Him. He restrained Himself from stopping the crucifixion (remember Gethsemane) and from coming down off of the cross -- something He was taunted with by His assailants. The angels were restrained (think of that, enough power to restrain the heavenly host) from fighting to prevent or avenge His mistreatment at our hands. The Father watched from heaven being fully self-restrained, for no other power could restrain Him, as His only Son was horribly abused by a very puny creation. God daily, moment by moment, resists the temptation (poor choice of words perhaps) to end all of this miserable activity taking place on His footstool. Every time we sin, it is the power of Divine restraint that allows us the opportunity to repent. However, the day is coming when the power of Divine restraint will be lifted. No man knows the hour, but all men can be sure it will happen. Holy restraint will one day end and then all men will see Him as He is. I am personally grateful for the countless demonstrations of His restraint where I am concerned. The power to restrain limitless power. Only God, whose love is greater than all our sin, could or would do such an incredible thing! Be thankful. Give praise. He is worthy!

I suspect that there is much we could learn from this self-restraining God about our own violent tendencies when we are abused. Restraining oneself is much harder than going after an offender who deserves our wrath. Yet, if we have a mind to be like God, we will need to exercise a great deal of self-restraint in our dealings with those around us. It has nothing to do with the worth of the offender and everything to do with the goodness of the offended. Goodness just naturally restrains violent responses. Any old run-of-the-mill sinner can respond in kind without even thinking. It takes an incredible individual, though, to respond in a manner that is kind. Perhaps we should turn some of our energies inward to discern and deal with some of our own unrestrained tendencies. It seems to me that the world is in need of examples of restraint far more than it needs loose cannons. Restraint provides opportunity for an offender to change, something that can never happen when we cast off all self-restraint at being poorly treated. I am so grateful that our Lord was not a divine loose cannon. His restraint led to my salvation. I wonder if something good might come of our restraint in times of turmoil. It takes a strong person to overcome their own strength for the sake of one who is weak. So let's live stronger toward ourselves than we do toward those who afflict us with pain and problems. Be a master of the skill of self-restraint!

# CHAPTER 20

## THE CLUTCH OF THE CURRENT

We were seeing the first fruits of our labors in our first pastorate and the need to baptize these three new converts gave me a sense of fulfillment in the scarce field that I worked in for Jesus. The church did not have a baptismal tank, and there were no swimming pools available. With no lakes nearby, I opted for the river that flowed through the community. The Trinity River is, or was at that time, a serious ribbon of water with a lot of rocky rapids, and it took some searching to find a spot that might work. The beach was a bit rocky, the water was not too deep, and we were about 300 yards above the rapids that churned nearest us downstream.

As I waded into the river, I was struck with the cold, the rocky bottom, and most disconcerting of all was the current that was stronger than it had looked from shore. But not to be deterred from this moment of success and glory, I made it to where the water was about hip deep, bracing myself against the current, facing the rapids just downstream from us. After a few shouted words of praise addressed to the small group on shore, striving to override the sound of the rapids, I called for the first candidate for this cold dunking.

My first victim was a young Native American girl of about 18 years of age. She was very short, perhaps maybe 5 feet tall and was, well, a substantial individual. One of the men in the church escorted her out to me and then made his way back to shore. With a couple of words of encouragement to her and then her brief testimony shared but probably not heard, it was time for my first official baptism as lead pastor in a small rural community. So I proclaimed, "in the name of the Father and the Son and the Holy Spirit I now baptize you into Christ" and I laid her over backwards. She lost her footing and the current took over from there.

I found myself struggling to hold on to my new convert, and the current quickly snatched her from my hands and off she bobbed toward the treacherous rapids just yards away. If not for a couple of quick men who ran down the shore line a bit and dove in to retrieve her, I fear she would also have been my first funeral. Once safe on shore and order being reestablished, I went back to my position and called for the next person. No one stood or answered. I called again and motioned for them to come but got no response. I waded back to shore and arranged to have a stout man wade out with me and stand just about four feet downstream facing me, and then we proceeded with baptizing the other two fearful candidates. Man, was I glad when that was over, though I suspect my jubilation about the dunking being completed was not anywhere near that of the three new kingdom kids.

I have faced a number of similar situations not with baptisms but with life itself that have taught me a lesson or two about how quickly the world and the enemy can snatch the things that matter the most in our lives away from us. No matter how well we brace ourselves, the worldly current that surges through this life can be quick to claim a Kingdom Prize and carry it into the destructive rapids of sin, pain, and loss. A moment of joy and victory has a way of becoming an hour of agony and despair that could have been prevented by well-placed and maintained relationships.

One of the lessons learned is that close capable companions are a lifesaver, literally. In Proverbs 18:1 the Scripture speaks of the foolishness of isolating or separating ourselves from those who can sustain us in trouble. This life will continually grasp at what you hold on to that is dear and precious, and fighting the current alone is one of the more foolish stands we can take. No matter how much preparation and planning, it is always wise to have capable people around us to help prevent our loss, or in some cases to help us retrieve our precious things before they are swallowed by the harsh rapid churning of this broken world.

I have thought very often of that first baptism and have always been thankful for those who kept my moment of victory from becoming a life-breaking hour of calamity. I had no idea going into that event the role that would be played by those who I saw as mere spectators. There are few spectators in the reality of life, just those who are placed by our Lord to provide a potential force that can snatch back what the currents of life have pulled out of our grip. We should also recognize that we have been placed in the lives of others to be available to plunge into the cold current to save the things that the Kingdom has given to our fellow servants.

God's relationship strategy is often somewhat soft in our lives. It is usually up to us to recognize and honor those who sit on the shore, just being there should the current get the better of us, people who have no idea the role they will play in a time of need, folks who care and only need the opportunity to manifest what God has given them for us. So honor those who sit quietly by the side. You just may need them to take an icy plunge into a strong current to save a prize that has been stripped from your hands.

# CHAPTER 21

## THE QUEEN OF HEAVEN - OR SO SHE SAYS

During the second year of my second pastorate, as a young minister of about 30 years of age I was invited to join the elite group of young men that were the inner circle of a woman who claimed to be the queen of heaven. On that particular day, I was in the office of our very run down and much-in-need-of-being-razed church when I heard the front door to the church open. I walked out into the sanctuary to see who had entered. What I found was a woman of perhaps 50 years in a wheelchair that was being pushed by a young man about my own age, and he was followed by five other young men of similar age. As we approached each other, I introduced myself as the pastor of the church, and she in turn introduced herself as the queen of heaven and went on to say that she had a message for me. But before sharing the message, she explained that she had no real need of the wheelchair, but because she had such high attainment in spiritual things the wheelchair served to impose a small amount of humility upon her lest she become exalted above measure.

Her message to me was that God had told her that I was to be the seventh young man needed to finalize her personal entourage and that I was to turn the church over to her. I glanced at the six young men following her and noticed that they were all about my age and build, they were all dressed exactly alike with dark suits and red ties, and even their haircuts were identical. For a brief moment, I was stunned at the strange and bold nature of what I had been told. Then, sensing the presence of the Holy Spirit, I replied, "Well, God has not said anything to me about that so I guess it's not going to happen." A brief but meaningless disagreement followed and then she signaled the young man who was pushing her chair, and they all turned and left without a word from any of her followers being spoken the whole time. I stood there wondering, "What was that all about? And did she really think I would just give my entire life to her?"

I have pondered that scenario for decades and have come to a couple of conclusions.  First, that so-called queen of heaven was moved by an evil spirit or perhaps many such spirits, and, yes, there are as many today as there were in Jesus' day.  Secondly, for reasons I have no explanation for, I had been pointed out to her as a target or a goal of some kind.  It took me some time to adjust to the idea that I was, for some reason, a specific target on the enemy's radar.  Since that day I have had other similar encounters with people who had heard a god tell them that they were to take over the church I pastored and that I was to follow them.  Add those encounters to the number of bogus prophetic words spoken to or over me, and you come up with a continual stream of the spiritually false that has sought to draw me into its depths.

The longer I live, the more spiritually dark works of the enemy manifest themselves both in multitude and in magnitude and both in and out of the church.  While I feel as though I have done a reasonable job of avoiding those tar pits of evil I am aware that they serve to cast a greater shadow over the true works of our Lord Jesus Christ and His Holy Spirit.  I hear with regularity prophecies, teachings, and revelations from professing Christians of no small experience things that make me shudder.  Even more distressing is the level of adeptness that they demonstrate with the Scriptures.  In fact, many of them know the Scriptures as well or better than I do. It is not a lack of that type of knowledge that is at the root of this evil.  It is, in my opinion, a lack of knowledge of the voice, the presence of God in the person of His Spirit, the character of God, and the very nature of God itself.

It is no wonder that Peter said, "Be sober, be vigilant; because your adversary the devil walks about like a roaring lion, seeking whom he may devour." I Peter 5:8 (NKJV) The warnings in Scripture of the false prophets, apostles, teachers, and so forth are abundant. We hear of doctrines of demons in the Lord's church and of light that is darkness in reality.

So be careful about listening to prophets and teachers whose lives you know nothing of personally. Draw close to church leaders who have proven their relationship to the Lord as being beyond question and turn away from the multitude of voices that cloud the very air we breathe. Remember the exhortation, "**know** those who labor **among** you." 1 Thessalonians 5:12 (emphasis added by me).

The times are evil as the Scriptures declare them to be. So be well anchored in relationship to solid Christian leaders and avoid following after the latest media voice or spiritual guru. Shun the latest craze or fad in ministry and cling to that which has proven to be good in the Lord.

# CHAPTER 22

## HURT AND WAITING

At six years of age I was as curious as most any other boy of my age and time.  It was hard to pass up a rock or old piece of plywood without turning it over to see what had taken up residence under it. I had a friend  my age who was as curious and full of energy as I was, and it was normal for us to take off without a destination (or telling our parents) to see what we could find.  Our attentions were easily captured by bugs, beetles, worms, and other crawly things, as well as lizards and frogs and -- did I mention lizards?

On one summer day, living in a small Oregon coastal community, we set off following our imagination, forgetting to tell our parents and crossing the forbidden main road in town to climb a long and steep hill.  We needed to see what was up there and explore the unseen side of the hill.  There were snails and slugs and long bugs with more legs than we could count.  What an incredible treasure we found as we poked and prodded and picked up creatures just for a closer look.  Eventually we were dragged out of our world by the realization that we had been gone for quite some time and our parents were most likely looking for us with assault weapons such as switches and belts.  An AK47 sounded like a decent grade on a spelling test at that time, but a willow switch was nearly lethal.

As we returned to the edge of the top of the hill that was covered with large trees, we could look down the slope, and we both had the same idea;  let's see how fast we can run down this hill.  My friend took off first, and I stood and watched as he flew down the steep grade, sliding to a halt at the edge of the main thoroughfare. He waved to me and yelled encouragement, so I went over the edge like I'd been shot out of a cannon.  The speed gained was such that keeping my feet up with my body became a major problem.  As I reached the bottom of the slope trying to apply all the brakes I had, I saw a black car on the road and it was on a collision course with me.  Somewhere about there my memory ends.

I don't recall the actual collision that I had with that older 1950-something automobile, but I do know that I did no real damage to it. I, however, went to the hospital, something else I have no memory of. What I do remember is laying at home on the couch after being released from the hospital and being told not to get up and no playing for a few days because I had a concussion (that was a big word I did not understand at the time). I was hurt, cut off from my friend and the activities I so loved, and waiting until things changed. Of all of that, the waiting just might have been the most painful part.

I began to complain about not having anything to do and my step dad said if I would be quiet and patient he would get me a toy. Please understand, my toys to date were pretty much some blocks of wood, bottle caps and my imagination. The promise of a toy was huge. And he expected me to wait and be quiet and be patient! Well, I did that for almost 10 minutes and then I began to press for the promise. It wasn't long before I was waiting, being quiet, being patient, and in trouble. I could not fathom the command to "Wait." Honestly, I still have trouble with that one. Anyway, my complaints prompted my overseer to leave angrily for the store and return with my first ever playdough. The problem was that his anger as he threw it at me robbed me of something. Not the playdough, but the gift I most wanted, the good will of my guardian, for without that my brand new playdough was lacking in the fulfillment that I had expected.

It seems that being quiet and patient and waiting are qualities that even God requires of His kids. And I still don't like it or do well at it. So what I have learned is that waiting is for us a form of connection to the extended goodwill of our Father who gives us all things, in due season. I still do not understand the waiting thing. But I do know it is there and it has something to do with what our Father has planned but come on already! Let's have the promise and forget the quiet and the patience thing. When you throw in the fact that many times we are in a state of pain when we receive the injunction to wait, it gets pretty near impossible for us.

Did I just mention the word "impossible"? God specializes in the impossible. I however, do my best to avoid it. I suspect at this time in my journey that our involvement in the impossible, or the possibility of it, excites God. I can just hear Him, "Come on, little man, you can do it. I know you can. I am right here. Just trust Me and do the impossible as you look at Me." When we can overcome our pain and find excitement in the promise before it arrives, we stir up something very Fatherly in our God. His pleasure affords an abundance that makes the arrival of the promise more thrilling than the promise itself; and considering His promises, that's saying something! And He won't throw it at you as if He has done some difficult and wearisome task on your behalf. It is His joy to give good gifts, things that far outshine blocks of wood and bottle caps.

So learn to embrace the wait. Embrace it in quiet patience, knowing that the wait serves to open the door to the abundant pleasure of our Father as we receive the gift in its time and for its purpose. "They that wait upon the Lord..."

# CHAPTER 23

## LAST SECOND ETERNITY

My brother and I were pastoring in two different communities in Northern California in 1978 when we got word that our mother was in a hospital in Washington State in a coma and not expected to recover. I had no money and not enough credit to make the trip to Washington to see her, but my brother flew up to be with her in her final moments. He related to me the following events as he experienced them in the last hours of our mom's life.

Mom was not, and to our knowledge had never been, a Christian. She had lived a hard life and was dying in her early 60s as a result. When my Brother Jerry arrived at the hospital and entered her room, he sat in a chair next to her bed. She was in a coma and unresponsive to any stimuli. His first concern was her lack of faith in Christ Jesus, and he leaned over toward her and said something like, "Mom, if you can hear me, I am going to pray a prayer, and I want you to think the words that I say." He then prayed a short and simple salvation prayer to receive Jesus as Savior and Lord.

Jerry then leaned back in his chair, and in just a couple of minutes our mom opened her eyes, looked at him and said, "Read me the Bible," and then slipped back into her coma. Though shocked at this unexpected turn of events, my brother opened a Bible to the book of Psalms and read to her for a time. Not long after he stopped, Mom again opened her eyes and said with emphasis, "Read me the Bible," and again dropped back into a coma. So, once again, Jerry turned to the Psalms and began to read and continued to do so for quite some time. He was eventually interrupted by mom as she awoke from her coma for the last time and said to him, "It's okay you can stop now and call the doctor. I see Jesus." She then slipped from this world into the waiting arms of the One who had been patiently waiting on her for her entire life as she lived without Him until the last moment before entering eternity.

65

Mom had done a lot of wrong in her life. She had endured a lot of pain and mistreatment as well. I do not remember her as being affectionate or gentle. My impression to this day, is that she was stressed, and life was robbing her of any real joy. She seemed to be just existing without any real purpose, and she never seemed to find a man who really loved her. She had spent her entire life in pursuit of things like alcohol to blur and soften the burdens of day-to-day life, and at the end that lifestyle claimed her body. As near as I can figure, Jesus just waited on her for her entire life, and then at the last second when she turned to Him, trapped in the prison of a coma, He welcomed her home, ushering her into eternity and His presence, and she went with great peace and joy.

I have wondered what it is that causes us to resist all the love and grace that God has poured out for us. And how is He able to wait with patience on we who trample on His love continually? I am very grateful that my brother had the presence of mind to reach out to her while she was in a coma. I don't know if I would have done that. I can't explain how she just woke up those three times and then dropped back into the darkness of a comatose state and yet had awareness in that black hole. I am just thankful that Jesus met her there and that one day I will get some answers, and maybe Mom and I can find the relationship that I feel we missed.

God works at levels, in places, and ways that we cannot comprehend. For this reason we need to allow the Spirit of the Lord to quicken our imagination about the possibilities when all appears to be over. I tend to think that imagination is one of the higher gifts that God has given to mankind. It is usually at its peak in children and seems to be why He is so drawn to them. It is perhaps one of the few things that will allow us to enter into an experience with God that may not be understood or embraced by many but gives us a fresh level of spiritual sight in Jesus. Who would have thought before it happened that Jesus would walk on water or that He would wait purposely for Lazareth to die before going to help him. We need to remember that Jesus has told us that there are things prepared in eternity for us that exceed our wildest attempt to imagine the unimaginable.  Maybe there is a strange sense of divine reasoning in our departing from the normal human reasoning at times when something is wrong or someone is hurting.

You may sometimes find yourself facing something that reason says is over or is beyond the reach of your attempts.  When you are there, remember to give the Spirit of Christ your imagination and maybe you will find yourself doing what seems unreasonable to others but is well within the reason of the divine and Holy One.  Who knows what God can do with a quickened imagination in a time of trouble.  As the song says, "I can only imagine".

And finally, if faith can move a mountain, then we need the imagination to try it that faith might work its wonders.  Perhaps faith is tied to imagination in some mysterious way.  It's hard to imagine isn't it?

# CHAPTER 24

## THE UNKNOWN REMEMBERED

We had been pastoring our second church for about three years when I received a phone call at home one evening. On the other end of the line was a male voice who identified himself simply as Dave, and I had no idea who he was. He said that he and I had a mutual friend and that friend had suggested that Dave give me a call to talk about his situation. I agreed to meet him in a cafe over coffee in the morning to hear his story.

I arrived at the cafe a few minutes early, found a table, sat down, and ordered a cup of coffee. It was just a couple of minutes later that I saw a man I did not know enter the cafe and something strange began to take place within me. There was a familiar sensation, like a surge in the presence of the Lord, and as I watched the man begin to look around the coffee shop I suddenly remembered a lot of things that I had never known. Or at least that is what it felt like. There was a small flood of information suddenly in my mind that I was absolutely sure of, only it was new information in my memory from some source other than my life and experience. Along with this remembered unknown information, there was an awareness of the voice of the Spirit of the Lord, that in an instant directed me as to what I needed to say and why this meeting was taking place.

I stood and waved to the man that I now knew to be Dave, he waved back and walked to my table. As we shook hands I quickly spoke first and told him not to say a word. I wanted to do all of the talking first, and then when I was done I would listen to his story. His expression showed some perplexity but he agreed. He then ordered coffee and our one and only meeting began.

I shared with him the following information, my memory of it now being a bit foggier than it was on that morning many years ago. I told him that he was married and had two teenage daughters. I spoke of his employment in law enforcement and how much he enjoyed doing that for a living. I reminded him that he was originally from Los Angeles, California, and while living there he had met the Lord Jesus and become involved in charismatic Christian church that had been a good experience. I then told him that his trouble began when the Lord called him to the ministry and he wanted nothing to do with it. In his resistance to that call he had moved away from all of the people who knew of it and he had buried that information deep in his soul, not sharing it with others trying to avoid being faced with it constantly. I spoke of his feelings of guilt and the undercurrents of turmoil that he kept hidden, even from his own family. Then I told him that I knew he had prepared a version of this story to tell me hoping that I would give him advice that would relieve his conscience of the burden of God's denied call on his life.

His expression was one of surprise and a bit of fear. He never said a word during all of this. He just sat there listening to me recite from my memory his memories. After a brief pause, I continued, telling him that it was time to go back. Back to Los Angeles. Back to the church he had skipped out on. Back to his old job. And I told him that he needed to go back and pick up the call that he was running from, get the training he needed, and then he could move forward with his life in Christ. When I stopped talking we were shrouded in a screaming silence that was obviously painful to Dave.

It took him a few minutes to be able to speak, and when he did he didn't say much. Just before he spoke I could see the clearing on his countenance of the barriers he had erected to the Lord. He then just nodded his head, told me that I was right, and that he would do what I had told him to do. We stood, shook hands, and parted ways. I have not seen or heard directly from Dave since that day. I did hear through our mutual friend that Dave had indeed gone back and picked up the discarded pieces of his former life, enrolled in a discipleship training school, and pursued the ministry.

The Scriptures tell us that the gifts and callings of God are irrevocable. Those divine impartations become instantly anchored in our own soul and spirit, and nothing we do can set us free from their claim on our lives. God doesn't so much ask us if we will; He just imparts His will in these things into us and then begins to provide a sense of direction or personal mission to bring focus to these gifts and callings. When we run from them or try to ignore them, they become an uncomfortable burden that can drain the meaning out of the rest of our lives. Most of the time we will walk a path that will carry us through a share of pain and suffering that accompanies these gifts and callings. And the only place where we find fulfillment is in embracing these divine grafts that provide a lens for every other portion of our lives.

In my own life, there were times early on when I would sit in the middle of the night and weep because of a kind of pain brought on by the presence of these heavenly needs within me and their demand to be met. I have not enjoyed many of the things that have come over the years as a result of His call on my life, but I have always found a fulfillment in that call that nothing else offered. There is in this call a bond with Christ that is found nowhere else. We become a partaker of His suffering as we face the challenges and conflicts that come our way in the service of the Cross. Most start out thinking about how great things will be only to find some very difficult and painful paths laid before them. This pain separates the called from the curious. It provides depth to the divine purpose.

There are many who try to ignore His call, or like Dave and Jonah flee it. But they never outrun it as it is always there ahead of them wherever they flee to. And God will always provide a way back for those who fled. It might be a giant fish, or a servant of the Lord who has memories of things never experienced or known, but the path back on track will find the prodigal of God's call.

Embracing the call is not simply doing it as Jonah did. It is investing your person into it. To embrace the call of God we must commit our all to it and arrange the rest of our lives around it. Those who do not know this call will never truly comprehend what the called experience and the called should not expect them to. There is an old adage that says that God does not call the equipped but rather that he equips the called. That equipping process can be difficult and in reality never stops for the call tends to be progressive for most. What is on our immediate horizon is only one of many scenarios to come. Each time we gain from our obedience a bit more of Him, we set off on another adventure that will demand more but will provide more.

The call is a high and holy privilege that comes with its own purpose and peculiar expressions. If you should be one of those whom the Lord calls, lay hold of it with all of your strength. It will be beyond your ability, but He will enable you to grow into it. The call of God is a special place of trust in divine things and ways. It gives more than it takes. Embrace it. It will embrace you whether you embrace it or not.

# CHAPTER 25

## I THOUGHT IT WAS FUNNY

I had no real friends in the eighth grade, partly because I was new to the area and the school. But in all honesty, I was not the warmest personality to come along. I was a loner, and I truly did not know much about being friendly. So it was a big deal to me when one of the other eighth grade boys whose parents owned a large cattle ranch in the area invited me over for a weekend. This is the first overnighter with a friend that I remember. I was both excited and anxious.

One of the things we did the first afternoon of my time with this new friend was to go exploring on a large tract of land owned by his family. We discovered what could only be a long-abandoned and falling-down line shack that we investigated. The only thing inside of interest was a small, perhaps 5 lbs. or so, wooden keg that was held together by some old rusty wire wrapped around the outside and sealed on both ends with round wooden lids. When we pried it open, we were surprised to find some very old black powder. Boy, was this a find! We knew exactly what to do with this unspent ordnance. We went outside the shack and poured most of the powder into a pile and used a small amount to make a trail about three feet long that we could light the end of and run. My friend just happened to have a small lighter that he carried so it would be his to light while I watched from a safer distance of perhaps 20 feet or so, feeling disappointed that I did not get to light the fuse. What took place is still pictured in my mind.

He thumbed the small lighter into life, then glanced at me, and we were both all smiles. He leaned over to touch the flame to the end of the small trail of powder and WHOOF! There was a huge cloud of blue white smoke that mushroomed into the sky the instant the flame touched the end of our ignition switch. Along with the cloud there was a flash of heat and light that lasted only a second. My friend, still kneeling where he lit the fuse turned my direction blinking his eyes as the hair of his head that hung over his forehead along with his eyebrows and lashes all floated to the ground having become instant ash. His face was red and filled with terror. I looked, blinked, and began to laugh uncontrollably. Somehow, he wasn't laughing. This was better than I had imagined. And then he said the magic words, "What am I going to tell Mom?" Now we were both in a panic because there would be no hiding what had happened to his face.

We survived the exposure to his parents with a lengthy lecture from his mom and nods with smiles from his dad. The real tragedy for me came the following Monday morning at school when he called me names and disowned me in front of the rest of our classmates. My laughter had become his pain. It was funny to me, and I have wished that I had a video of that day's event. But because it was no fun for him, what I thought was funny he thought was humiliation, and our friendship was shipwrecked. I suffered his attacks for a long time after that little incident. It made me resolve to not have friends anymore. Our breach was never healed, and I don't know what ever happened to him. I know that I processed a lesson from that experience.

Laughing with someone is far different than laughing at them. When there is a personal expense to be paid for something, it should be discounted as fun whether it is funny or not. I can still react to things that happen suddenly to someone with a laugh, but I try to quickly determine the expense they paid for my humour. When someone is suddenly launched into a place of pain and fear what they really need is a friend to help them deal with the internal flash that they have experienced.

We as people tend to degenerate sometimes in situations that cost others. Somehow those things just get to us. Come on, you found this story funny too. But he will never hear you laugh, so you are safe and so is he. I have missed that friendship far more than I enjoyed that moment of laughter. But alas, as my father in law would say, "You can't push water back up under a bridge." So the next best thing is to learn from what happened and adjust for a better result in the future.

Be careful when you laugh at someone. There is a vulnerability built into those settings that is hard to recover from. Perhaps had the relationship been older and stronger things might have ended differently. But as it is, my laughter became his pain which in turn became my pain, and we both lost in the end. And I really thought that was funny.

# CHAPTER 26

## THE WAX APPLE

This chapter is going to be different than the rest. It is something of a concern to me, since I would hate to see those I love fall for the wax apple. A wax apple is a lovely replica of the real thing, but without taste or goodness.

As I have mentioned elsewhere in this book, I grew up unfamiliar with love and affection. Long before I became a teenager, I stopped expecting affection and prepared myself for hostility and rejection. There was a level of tolerance, but it could never be mistaken for affection or love. My presence seemed to be tolerated as long as I didn't bother the household powers present. Even my behaviors were tolerated as long as they did not impose on the wishes of my parents. I knew from a fairly early age the difference between tolerance, the wax apple, and love, they are not equal.

Through the years as a Christian and as a pastor, the topic of love has been ever present, though the demonstration of it may have at times been lacking. I think that I have seen two different love movements in Christianity to date with a third one in full bloom. While each has a different flavor due to the prevailing cultural norm, they are yet all very much alike to me. The standard raised is to love the unlovely who may be in full rebellion to the status quo. I am all for that, by the way. The problem is that what is most often meant is not to love them but to be (overly) tolerant of their behavior so they will feel comfortable around us. That is tolerance, the wax apple, not love. In almost no other setting would we advocate that manner of treatment for these wounded people whom Jesus truly loves.

In a marriage, there are behaviors that will not be tolerated whether one is loved or not. We have no problem expecting monogamy from our spouse. Because we do love them, we have no intention of tolerating behavior to the contrary. Every loving parent refuses

75

to tolerate a wide range of behavior from their children simply because they do love them. So here is the bomb, unconditional toleration, the wax apple, is contrary to unconditional love. The former destroys the latter. Unconditional love, as Jesus demonstrated it, says things like, "Go and sin no more," or "You make void the command of God by your traditions," or "How long must I put up with you, oh you of little faith," or "Get these things out of here (spoken in anger) for my Father's house will be called a house of prayer, but you have made it a den of thieves." All of this and much more from the One who is Love by very nature. Notice His nature is love, not tolerance. These two are not equal and do not represent the same things.

All men should be treated with dignity and love, but not all lifestyles and behaviors should be tolerated. Love at its best helps the loved one out of his or her brokenness so that they can rise above their own failures. That is not just the work of Jesus; it is the work of every servant who loves Him (remember He said, "You go and teach them everything I taught you"). Love is never content to leave a wounded person untreated, just trying to prevent further wounds. Love does both, it heals the wound and alters the lifestyle that causes the wounds. Jesus died to both free you from your past sins and to free you from a lifestyle of sin, and only then are you free.

Tolerance tends to be a worldly substitute for love. Just let everyone be and get along, the tolerant says. It doesn't matter what they do as long as you love them, he declares. How many rapists or murderers should change? Tolerance says none. Love says all. How many alcoholics and drug users should change? Tolerance says none. Love says all. I could go on and on here. It is my evaluation according to the things I have seen over the years that absolute tolerance becomes total rebellion and is by nature destructive.

Some seem to be of the opinion that being sensitive to a person means zero confrontation. I think that sensitivity means

76

confrontation where it is needed with compassion. Sensitivity is really "having the sense of what is happening," not ignoring it so they won't feel bad.

My desire as I write this is that all of my tribe should know true love and affection and understand that unrestrained and hurtful behavior will not be tolerated. Love one another, but do it with the best interest of the other in mind. Love one another, and be open to each other, even if some do a poor job on the compassion end. Love one another as Mom and I have demonstrated it to you. In this manner, you will show that you truly love the Lord your God and He will be pleased. Toleration is what we are left with when love fails. Do not make the mistake of thinking of them as the same or as being in any way equal. If you do, you just might find yourself with a mouthful of wax apple.

# CHAPTER 27

## CAPTURE THE DEER

I was 13 years old and my older brother Jerry was 16 or so, and we were out exploring the area around a lake that was a mile or so from where we lived. A very thin sliver of land with barbed wire fence running down the middle of it protruded into the lake for a hundred yards or so. We noticed a young spotted fawn on this sliver of land between us and the main lake body but on the opposite side of the fence. That is when my brother got the idea that we needed a pet deer, kind of like in a Walt Disney movie we had seen.

The fawn was on the opposite side of the fence from where we stood and was obviously nervous. My older brother's idea was that he would make his way down the fence line past the fawn and cross through the fence to the side the fawn was on, and then chase the fawn back toward me. That would be my signal to also cross through the fence and be ready to capture the small creature, holding onto it until he arrived to help subdue our new and quite cute pet. A simple straightforward strategy. I was ready.

Once we were both in place, Jerry started toward the fawn, and the fawn started toward me at full speed as I stood next to a fence post to be invisible. As the high-speed fawn neared my position, I leapt out and tackled it with both it and me tangling up together in a scrambling ball on the ground. It was about then that I discovered that a fawns hooves are actually rather sharp and their legs move way faster than my hands. Getting ahold of that miserable little creature proved to be easier than getting away from it. I did manage in short order to get free of that slashing little buzz saw but not before I had a few cuts in both my clothes and my body. The fawn got its feet on the ground and sped away nonetheless for wear. I was just gaining my feet and taking stock of my battle wounds when my brother ran up wondering why I didn't hang on to it. Really? Needless to say, we went home without the new pet, but with a healthy respect for those violent little forest animals that everybody loves. No wonder man took up hunting.

I suspect just about everybody has tried something just as foolish as trying to capture a deer and with about the same results. I discovered in this little adventure that the cuteness of a spotted fawn is in direct proportion to the distance between it and the observer. This equation, by the way works, for a lot of things in life. From a distance, an incredible photo, but get too close and you discover what the word "wild" really means. It seems as though we as people have a default where some types of learning or knowledge are concerned. We make assumptions based on our desire more than on the reality of what is staring us in the face. We even lay out whole strategies to get our wish accomplished. But all too often our desire becomes a battle of nightmarish proportions, and getting out is never as easy as getting in.

I suspect that as you are reading this little lesson in life that you may have a time or two come to mind where you tried to do something as off the chart as collecting a new and cute pet the hard way. Yours might have been something like a new car you just couldn't live without or inviting a homeless guest into your home. It might have looked like the perfect job or the perfect vacation, or even the perfect person to date, desirable at first but "wild" in a way that made you work to let go, leaving you with a few reminders that would be around for a while and that might even produce a scar or two.

The really good thing about these kind of experiences is when they end you can then claim to have achieved a worthy level of wisdom to pass around to the foolish children who can't tell a deer from a buzz saw. I have recovered from the trauma of that day, and I actually enjoy watching young deer wander around my yard in the early morning. I no longer hold on to the animosity that I had so long ago and I find those little four- legged critters to be once again cute, in a wild sort of way. So, before you play capture the deer, or the job, or the spouse, or whatever, you may want to seek some advice from someone who has been there and survived to tell about it. Or you could just go ahead and do it, and if you survive, you could be the one others don't bother to ask or listen to. It's your life and therefore your choice, so have at the little buzz saw, but don't say I didn't warn you.

# CHAPTER 28

## MEETING THE CHALLENGE

In the fall of the year that I turned 16, my girlfriend's parents invited me to go along with the family on a long weekend to the California coast to do some camping and ocean fishing. I had to buy my first fishing license to do this at the unbelievably high price of $3.50, but it did include both freshwater and saltwater fishing, so it was worth it. I bought a brand new very stout six-foot fishing rod with a large bait casting reel for a few dollars more and I was set. Our destination was Fort Bragg and though it would be cool, well to the point of frosty at night, the tent I slept in was sufficient for me. Adventure awaited.

Upon waking up on our first morning there, we discovered a thin layer of ice on the water bucket. Unusual but not dramatic, until I was told to break the ice and wash up. That was dramatic. Following breakfast, we went out fishing and discovered the tide to be out quite a long way, so we made our way out to some very large rocks that were in the shallows of the water, climbed up, and began fishing. After a couple of hours with nothing to show for our time, we noticed that the water had risen significantly. We would need to wade, while waves crashed in, back to shore in water that was about three feet deep. This was the second challenge (the wash up in ice water being the first) of the trip, but no problem for a 16-year-old that wanted to be thought of as a man. We managed to drag our drenched selves to the shore without a major incident, so it was back to camp to dry out and eat.

Later that afternoon while walking on a beach with my girlfriend, I kept eyeing a sheer rock cliff that was covered with some sort of green vines. It was perhaps 80 feet to the top and would have been impossible to climb, but for the vines. For some strange reason, climbing to the top at the highest and most sheer point beckoned to me. It was a huge challenge filled with the element of danger and the opportunity to demonstrate to my girlfriend just how much of a man I really was. Finally, against her wishes, I walked to the cliff and began to pull my way up using the vines to grasp onto and gain altitude. I was in good physical shape, well-coordinated, and tenacious. I made it to the top without incident and stood surveying my deed. I had met the challenge and won!

By the time our vacation was ending and we were packing up to head for home, I was noticing a major rash breaking out all over me accompanied by an agonizing itch. When we finally reached home, I was swollen so bad that my foster parents took me to a doctor's office where the doctor diagnosed me with an extreme case of poison oak and prescribed some ointment and pills along with a shot. It was my first real encounter with this apocalyptic plague, and with my eyes fully swelled shut and even my tongue and throat swelled to where eating was almost impossible, I was as miserable as I could imagine being. But I had met the challenge. Against sensible advice. For no apparent reason. And with no one caring about it one way or another. So there I laid in misery, wishing that I had let that particular challenge pass me by. It seems strange to me how things so meaningless and dangerous and foolish can capture our attention and draw us into them against all sound reason. And yet we people, especially when we are young, tend to be drawn to things for the sole purpose of proving ourselves worthy.

There is a similar demand within our souls that searches for a challenge big enough to prove that we are worthy of God and His love. We can find ourselves doing all manner of work and labor in

82

an attempt to prove to God and to others that we are good and worthy of higher recognition and reward. Like my climb up the poison-oak-covered cliff, taking up the challenge to become good enough is foolish and without reward. For those of us who truly want to get it right and to make heaven, be it known that there is no challenge you can meet that will get you there.

You are not good. Get used to it. According to Scripture, no one is. God is good, and that is hard for we who are not good to get used to. Yet it is His goodness that meets our need, not our own. When it comes to true spiritual life, there is no cliff you can climb to find it, no challenge that will reward you with what you are looking for. If you take that course, you will find yourself sitting in misery wishing for something greater. Toss away all attempts to earn the love and grace of God, for those things are free for the asking. You don't have to meet that challenge as it was done for you by Jesus on Calvary's tree. Relax and embrace what He has done, and you will find that His work will become a well of life within you. Don't fall for the draw of a cliff to nowhere. Don't be deceived by the poison oak offer of assistance. Accept what Jesus Christ has done and celebrate the height that He has lifted you up to. And stop worrying about being good enough or up to the challenge. He took care of all of that for you. In Him, you are already there. This is the challenge worth taking up, putting your faith in the One who will always be faithful to you.

# CHAPTER 29

## A RESCUE GONE FOUL

Where we lived on farmland that was owned by the family who my step dad worked for, was a great place to spend my 13th year. We had a close neighbor who also worked for the farmer and he had a German Shorthair dog that was a nuisance but not in any way dangerous. He often followed us kids around whether we wanted him to or not and most of the time we didn't want him around. He chased away all of the rabbits and birds that we tried to catch and was just a general pest, not unlike some folks I have known.

On one occasion when I was out exploring I came across a full-grown skunk. That wasn't so unusual in itself, but this particular skunk seemed to want to follow me around. He never got within touching distance, but, boy, was he foul, and there didn't seem to be any escaping him. That was when that pesky dog of our neighbor's showed up, and things really began to escalate. That crazy dog took-after that big old skunk, and the whole country seemed to be clouded with the results.

The skunk wound up with his teeth firmly affixed to the dog's nose, and he had his body and legs literally wrapped all around that dog's muzzle. And before you knew it, the dog was laying on his side with all four legs kicking and whimpering something awful, and the skunk wasn't about to let go. I was pretty sure that the dog was gonna lose this one in a big way so I grabbed an old 2x12 that was about 12 or 14 feet long, stood it on end within reach of the two combatants, and let the end drop on the skunk. That did the trick. The skunk let go, and while he was dazed, the dog caught his breath and ran straight to me, only now I was running and screaming and trying to get rid of that nasty old hound who was most likely just showing his gratitude.  Should have let the skunk win.  I could have outrun him.

Sometimes helping another out of a problem becomes a problem. Please bear that in mind.  I'm not suggesting that you do not help others, just that you be ready for their misplaced and possibly overzealous gratitude.  You may find them quite under foot and hard to get rid of.  Helping others is a wonderful Christian thing to do.  We need to do that with regularity and all joy of spirit.  But we should not be so naive as to think that solving their problem is necessarily the end of the problem.

Jesus delivered the demoniac, and had to deal with the deep gratitude that the delivered had for Jesus.  On one occasion a mob was moved to take Jesus and make Him king by force as a way of expressing their gratitude.  This was a problem for Jesus as His crown had to come from His Father, not his followers.  By way of thanks, Paul and Barnabas found the crowd bowing down to worship them when they healed a person.  They were frantic to undo this act of gratitude.

It is not unusual for a rescue to become a problem.  We shouldn't be surprised by this.  It seems to be one way for the enemy to undo what Jesus has just done through us.  It can, if we let it, cause us to turn our backs on those whom the Lord puts in our path to help.  So be prepared whenever you extend a helping hand to meet with a problematic response by the rescued, often out of sheer gratitude. Don't quit because people make helping such a burden.  You did not help them just for their sake, but you did so as much for the Lord's sake, and you do not want to lose sight of that.

On a final note, do not quit helping because of a lack of gratitude or a lack of success. Again, you are doing this as much or more for Jesus' sake as for the one in need. Learn to look beyond the situation and into the eyes of Christ who has sent you to be His ambassador to the broken and hurting He has already died for. Don't let the foul odor that may cling to the rescued turn you from being a rescuer.

# CHAPTER 30

## UNDER THE INFLUENCE

When my wife and I were first married I was working as a civilian employee for the U.S. Navy at the Port Chicago Naval Weapons Station in Concord, California. This was during the end of the Vietnam War, and Port Chicago shipped roughly 70% of the bombs and ammunition that were used by the U.S. Military, there in Vietnam. There were a large number of employees that worked there on the docks 24-7, and several among them were drug users. I was not in that group. I was, however, acquainted with several who were a part of that group.

We were transported from the base to the docks in old stock trucks that had been fitted with benches around the inside perimeter and a narrow bench down the center. There were steel grab bars running overhead throughout the truck for those who did not have a seat to hold on to. We were taken to the docks in the morning in these trucks, then returned at lunch time to the base, then returned to the docks again and finally back to base at the end of each shift.

On one day as we were boarding the stock truck to head back to the docks after lunch, I was next to last in line to board. I stopped just inside the door in the crowded truck and grabbed a bar running overhead and watched as the last man in line boarded our transport. He was obviously under the influence of some sort of drug as he made his way carefully, seeming dazed and disoriented, onto the truck. He had a problem to solve, though. He held in one hand his hard hat and in the other an open orange soda, and as a result he could not hold on to the grab bar to keep from falling. I watched as he looked from one hand to the other appearing to find it difficult to come up with a solution to this problem. He finally bent over and carefully set his hard hat upside down on the floor of the truck at his feet, shifted the orange soda to the hand that had held the hard hat, reached up and grabbed a bar and was set to go.

Standing next to him I watched as he seemed to slip into a sleep of sorts. Then I noticed that the hand that held the orange soda was slowly lowering, right over his hard hat, and he unknowingly began to pour his orange soda into the hard hat, without spilling a drop on the truck floor. He must have poured more than half of his soda into the hat on the trip to the docks. When we arrived and the truck lurched to a stop, he woke up and gently picked up his hat, stepped off the truck and placed his hard hat on his head, pouring its entire contents all over his head without seeming to notice and strolled off to work. I headed off to my work site wondering how long it would take him to notice the sticky soda that was all over his head and shoulders, being glad that he was not on my work team. Being under the influence shuts down a lot of our natural awareness that keeps us safe and healthy.

I cannot count the times that I have sat with an individual, attempting to give them some advice on life, only to find that they were already under the influence of someone or something else, and nothing I said would penetrate the fog of that influence. More than once I counseled someone against a behavior that they would eventually wake up to, only to find it too late for them to avoid the trap associated with that behavior.

Being under an influence can be a good thing, if it is not a substance but is instead a mentor, or some such person who is solid in Christ and Christ's Word. But being under the influence of someone who is not solid in Christ and His Word can become a devastating experience at the least. Sometimes the influence can be as simple as a desire that we have that lacks wisdom and/or value.  Often people who have influence in our life have so because of a common identity with pain.  That is not a wholesome influence. You will find a multitude of people who would like to influence you. Being under the influence means that your way of thinking, feeling, and behaving are subject to another's ways.  So before you allow someone to become an influence in your life, be sure that what you see and hear of them is what you want to look and sound like.  Or you could just get used to wearing orange soda on your head and shoulders.

# CHAPTER 31

## THE DEMONIAC

Shortly after my wife and I moved to pastor our first church, we were woken up in the middle of the night by pounding on our front door. Upon answering it, I found a woman of perhaps 30-something standing there, and she was a bloody mess from head to toe. We ushered her in and asked what had happened, as we set about cleaning up her wounds. She told us a story of how her husband, (they were our next-door neighbors) had been beating on her and was threatening to kill her and how she had run from his brutality and made her way into a very thorny blackberry patch nearby to escape him. After a time, when she knew her husband had returned to the house, she had clawed her way out of the berry patch and come to our home as we were the closest neighbor out there in the country area we lived in. After cleaning her up and treating her wounds, we made the couch into a bed for her so we could all get some sleep.

The following morning at breakfast we agreed to give her a ride to the home of a friend of hers and I suggested that she consider getting a court restraining order against her husband to get some police protection as, according to her, this was not the first such episode between them by a long stretch. Before dropping her off she said that she would do that.

I received a call from her a few days later, asking me if I would meet with her and her husband, who I will call "Tom" here, to provide them with some marriage counseling. I agreed and we met at the church which was just in front of the parsonage that my wife and I lived in. Their home was to the side of the church. Our home was accessed by a dirt driveway between the church and their home. When I met Tom at this counseling session, I was a bit overpowered by his size. He was all of six and a half feet tall and must have weighed in at well over 300 pounds and though he had a beer belly, he was obviously a very strong and intimidating man. They were sitting in the front row in the sanctuary, and I sat on the wooden altar bench just in front of them, there being no office in this little church, and we began to talk. We had not been there very long when the front door to the small church opened and in walked a county sheriff's deputy who came up to us and asked if one of us was Tom. He had an official paper in his hand and when Tom identified himself to the deputy, I spoke up knowing what the deputy held in his hand. I said to Tom, "That is probably a restraining order, and I am the one who recommended it because of your violent abuse of your wife." Having served the restraining order, the deputy walked quickly out and drove off. A couple minutes later Tom walked out and drove off, saying nothing. That ended the only meeting I was to have with Tom that did not have violent intent on his part.

About that time my wife and I purchased a stereo record and eight-track player from the local Western Auto store. It proved to have problems, so I was taking it back with the assistance of a pastor friend from a mountain town a few hundred miles away. When we pulled to the curb across the street from the Western Auto store and began to unload the stereo, an older pickup truck pulled into the open lot to the side of my car, and Tom jumped out of the pickup and it was clear that he was mad. As I turned to face him, he stalked up to me and said, while pointing at me, "I want you!" As he got within reach of me, he swung his right fist in a wide powerful arc toward my head. I knew for certain that the next face I saw would be Jesus, so I raised both of my hands and extended them toward heaven while turning my face up as well. And then something out of this world began to happen. Tom's fist came to within a hair's width of my face and stopped. He then began to stumble backwards as if he was being dragged, and he began to shout and scream, "Leave me alone. You can't do this! Leave me alone!" He was dragged by the unseen force back until he was spread wide against his pickup, and there he struggled and yelled for a time as we watched in fearful fascination.

After a couple of minutes of this something or someone (The Holy Spirit) came over me, and I marched up to Tom and, pointing my finger up into his face, I began to tell him of the saving power of Jesus Christ and how he needed to give his life to Christ. When I had done that, Tom seemed to relax, his arms dropped to his side, and he said to me in a quiet voice, "Preacher, you have no idea just how powerful your God is." Then he got into his pickup and drove away.

Tom continued to make threats against my life and the lives of my wife and two very young daughters. He would build large fires in the middle of the night and fire weapons and yell threats to scare us. It worked better than it should have. I made it a regular practice to walk the property line between us and him every day for at least an hour praying in the Spirit. It was the only thing I could think of as a defense against this raging demoniac who terrified even the county sheriff's department. He was a drug dealer, among other things, and there were rumors that he had killed more than one person. To this day I believe those stories. There were a number of lesser encounters with Tom but the Lord was always faithful to protect me and my family from him. I prayed often for Tom and his salvation but did not know how to reach him, so I just walked my defense line in prayer, and left it to the Lord.

It was some months later on a Sunday evening at a prayer service in the church that Tom opened the church door in the middle of the service as all were at the altar praying and I was walking the platform in prayer. Tom walked, shaking violently all the way to the altar, and dropped hard on his knees at the altar. Everyone in the church had gone silent and looked at Tom and myself. I heard in that moment the clear voice of the Spirit of God tell me to lay a hand on Tom and command the demons to be bound and silent and to let Tom make his own decision about Jesus without their influence. I did that and as I did, Tom gave a huge gasp as if getting a breath of air for the first time in a long time. He stopped shaking and relaxed as he gently rocked back and forth on his knees, all the time looking into the palms of his hands and then looking around and then back at his hands. I waited to see what would happen.

After a time, Tom looked up at me as I stood at his side and he spoke to me. I don't remember the exact words but it went something like this, "Your God is real, and He is more powerful than you can know. I like to go to the big cities from time to time to find people on the street and strangle them. I like watching the light go-out of their eyes. My hands are bloody hands and though your God is real, I don't want to quit what I do." He then stood to his feet, turned and walked out of the church and pretty much out of my life.

Several years later I was talking with someone from that little rural community and I asked them about Tom. They told me that not long after my last encounter with Tom he had overdosed on a massive amount of over-the-counter pain drugs, killing himself.

I often encounter Christians who feel that serving God means you always succeed. But I have found that God always opens a door, but the person or people He is dealing with must be willing to step through it. Tom could have been saved that Sunday night, I am sure of that. But God left the decision to Tom. God gave him the liberty and peace to make a good decision, but Tom turned away, fully knowing what he was doing. I am always saddened when I think about Tom. But I did what I needed to, and he did what he wanted to, and God accepted both of our decisions.

Jesus could not convince the rich young ruler to give up his wealth, and that saddened Jesus. Paul couldn't convince Felix to follow Jesus, and I am sure that saddened him. Not all who hear will come in. But Jesus still invites them all. His invitation usually passes across the lips of a servant like me or you, some plain follower of His that will go wherever He asks us to go and do whatever He asks us to do. The invitation is always genuine. But the invited are not always inclined to accept. Some folks like Tom are very hard to deal with, but Jesus still loves them. Even though they are a drug dealing, people-killing demoniac, Jesus loves them and sends us to make the offer of eternal life. Some come; some do not. But all are invited. And Jesus' love for them can only be manifested through our love and faithfulness to Jesus, especially in the hard things. So go and extend the invitation. The rest is out of your hands.

# CHAPTER 32

## PERSONAL RISK

In 1980 we were pastoring a small church in the foothills in Northern California. Because the church was small, it was necessary for me to work a full-time secular job. I had landed work in a small mill that produced fence and fence products that were prefabricated. At one time my work-site was located about 50 feet from the large 8x12 glass window that gave the foreman Louis (not his real name) a view of most of the plant floor and the workers. He was somewhat of a slave driver, demanding production every moment of the day from the workers. He wasn't well-liked or respected.

Many of the employees of the company would set up pranks to be played on our overseer. The area where we lived and worked had a large population of poisonous rattlesnakes, and Louis was terrified of snakes. Louis kept a bicycle just outside of his office door to ride through the plant to keep an eye on the workers, making sure they stayed as busy as he wanted them to be. One day as a group of us workers sat at lunch outside, a very large rattlesnake crawled slowly into the circle of us men and we just watched him move into the middle, and then someone suggested that this could be an opportunity to prank Louis.

The snake was dispatched and carried to Louis' bicycle and tied to the upright supporting the bicycle seat with the head of the snake protruding out from under the seat along the bar that was on all boy's bikes of the time. Then it was just a matter of watching until Louis would come out of the office, jump on the bike, and head through the plant. Working close to the office I had a good view. Sure enough, Louis came out and grabbed his bike, threw his leg over, and gave a push and was off - briefly. He hadn't gone but about a hundred feet when he noticed his reptilian passenger and made an attempt to get off the bike, moving straight up into the air only to land hard on the concrete floor. The man that worked next to me was a major player in this prank and many other pranks on a number of people in the mill. I'll call him "Joe". Joe roared with laughter. The best prank yet.

Everyone knew that Joe was not to be trusted. He would nail your gloves to posts. Or maybe pack your thermos with fine wet sawdust. He would eat the goodies from your lunch or unplug your power tools. His imagination just never stopped. He was in his mid 20s and he was always in trouble with the law. He was a bit loud and brassy and had no real friends at the mill. I witnessed to him regularly and was made fun of by him as a result. One day I had had enough of his pranks. So when he set his metal lunch pail on the counter ready to be grabbed as he rushed out the door after work and was not looking, I opened it and nailed it to the counter, where it sat with two nails through the inside bottom of the pail. When the horn sounded that signaled it was time to go home, he raced by his pail, snatching it up as he passed, and made it out the door with only the handle of the lunch pail in his hand. The rest remained nailed to the counter. He knew I had done it, and while he complained he was smiling. It was like a strange sort of connection.

On a Monday morning not long after that, Joe came in rather down, which was unusual for him. He had gotten into trouble with the law over the weekend about something, and it had caused problems between him and his girlfriend. When he finally did speak to me, it was with a sense of pain, and he confessed that he did not like his life at all and wished that he could be different. Within just a few minutes, I asked him if he would like to kneel and receive Jesus as his Savior, and he said yes. So there we were on the cement at work, praying with the Foreman Louis watching out the big window. We both knew that Louis was watching, but we didn't care. This was too important, and if we lost our jobs that was okay. We would risk our employment for Jesus. Louis watched the whole time, not coming out to yell at us. When we were done, we stood and went back to work, and that's when Louis started out to talk to us. The plant manager had also been watching us, unbeknownst to us, and he intercepted Louis, and after a word with him, Louis went back into the office and never once mentioned our prayer time.

I don't know to this day what the plant manager said to the foreman, but his words most likely saved our jobs as the Word of the Lord saved Joe that day. It was at substantial personal risk that I prayed with Joe there, knowing what could and probably would happen. But there are times when the Kingdom agenda trumps the priorities of this world, even if it does cost us for obeying it. Jesus does not have a "no-risk" policy in His Kingdom. In fact, it can be very high risk. You can get crucified, among other things. In fact, we use that term, "crucified" as an expression of high personal risk and cost in day- to-day life. It kind of sums it all up. He was crucified for us, so we should not hesitate to return the act in love for Jesus. All Christians live at risk in this world all the time. We were promised by the Lord that the world would hate us just as it hated Him. In the end, one of the signs of Jesus' favor in this life is the world's rejection of us. So don't fear the risk; embrace it and, if necessary, pay the price. It's what Jesus would do. Did do, in fact.

Oh! And by the way, some-time later, Louis lost his wife to cancer. Guess who he sought out, in private, for prayer. Yep, that became my privilege also. Louis began going to church after that, not my church, but that didn't matter. The risk of a job was what it took to birth two souls into God's Kingdom. So take the risk!

# CHAPTER 33

## SOME EXPENSIVE EGGS

A new convert in our first church had told me of her stepfather who lived out in the mountains where he had a small ranch in a small valley there. He was a rather heathen sort and hated religion of all types, and for some reason she mentioned in passing that he sold eggs. In my prayer time a couple of weeks after she had told me this, I clearly heard the Lord tell me to go buy a dozen eggs from this man. Now, I am smart enough to know that this was not about eggs, and I was clueless as to just what Jesus had in mind, but I got the directions and went to buy a dozen eggs that I really did not need from a man who I did not know at a price that was ridiculous because that's how God works.

As I crested the last hill on this dirt road in the mountains, I could see the small ranch sitting there in the valley just below me. I pulled to a stop in front of the somewhat worn and dilapidated house and saw two men standing off to my left at a corral attached to a large barn. I got out of my car, walked to the two men and said, "I hear you sell eggs I need a dozen," just as if that was normal for me. The man nearest me, dressed in overalls and in serious need of a bath, haircut, and a shave peered at me and responded, "You're that new preacher in town, ain't ya?" Then, as he pointed toward the house, he went on speaking, "You see that shotgun on the porch yonder? Well if you can get out of here faster than I can get to that shotgun, then you get to leave. Otherwise, you'll be here for a very long time." And then he started for the house. I ran to my car, jumped in, started it, and spun a rooster tail of dust and gravel turning around and getting out of there. It has been my experience that sometimes God has bad ideas. This was one of those times.

Perhaps a week or so later while praying I again heard the voice of the Lord instruct me to go buy those eggs, only this time, He and I had differing opinions about those eggs. I argued for a time with the Lord, telling Him I didn't really like eggs all that much, they were cheaper in the local store and a lot closer, and that crazy old mountain man was dangerous. God didn't care much about my argument, and I soon found myself on my way back into the mountains for eggs I wanted nothing to do with. As I pulled in this time, there was just the one man, the owner of this hillbilly hideaway, standing at the corral looking at some stock, and the shotgun was right by his side. I took a deep breath, got out of my car, and walked to him and said, "I still need those eggs." He picked up the shotgun, clicked the safety off, and said, "You have one chance of leaving here, Preacher. I'm going to ask you a question and if you have the right answer you can have the eggs. If not, you're here to stay." Then came the question, "What does a person have to do to go to heaven?" Oh for crying out loud, Lord! I don't know how this madman's mind works. After a brief deliberation, I decided that if I was going to heaven today I wanted to do it with the truth on my lips, so I answered, "The Bible says you must be born again."

Then he smiled, set the shotgun down, and said, "That is the only answer I will accept." Then he invited me into his home for a cup of coffee, and so we went into the house. The door to the house was open, and there were a number of dogs and cats everywhere, even on the table and on the counter. Garbage lay scattered all over the house and flies filled the air along with a gagging odor. He swept a load of trash from the table in front of a chair with his arm and told me to have a seat, which I did, carefully. He then grabbed a used coffee cup off the counter, dumped out what was in it, wiped it out with his shirttail, blew into it, and then filled it with coffee and sat it down in front of me. He did the same for himself. Then he began to share with me how he had been raised in a Christian home and had turned his back on church and the Lord over some issue about the way people practiced religion, preachers being the worst of the lot. We drank our coffee, and I listened. He gave me the eggs, said I was welcome back anytime, and that He appreciated the chance to talk about the Lord. I do not know if he ever recommitted his life to Jesus, but I do know that the path to do so was cleared because of eggs.

We have no idea what is in another's past, but we can be sure that it has some impact on their present. And we can be fairly certain that it is affecting their future as well. God knows all of these things and he addresses them in people's lives through us, and things as simple as a dozen eggs. Often what God gives us is a direction toward something, much like he did with Abram, without any explanation, and it is up to us to move that way, discovering the purpose and goal enroute. So many lives are bound by their own past or another's failures, and setting them free from those things is what God is all about. Learn to listen to the voice of the Lord, and you will find yourself involved in the work of God in the lives of others. It won't normally be easy and quite often will not make sense, at least to start with, and it can even be dangerous and scary, but once the door is opened and you enter the problems of another's life, healing can start. So go and get those eggs, or whatever it is that is the key to another's prison cell, and let them out, in the name of Jesus!

# CHAPTER 34

## HUMILITY THE HARD WAY

One of the more often quoted, or misquoted verses in the Bible is from Proverbs 16:18. Most people reference this verse with the words, "Pride goes before a fall," which is a misquote, actually. It says that pride goes before destruction and a haughty spirit before a fall. Pride and a haughty spirit are two very different things. Pride is a condition of the heart or soul, while a haughty spirit is a temporary arrogant attitude brought on by a sense of success or an undo sense of self-worth due to a success. Pride in this text is to be avoided at all costs for it destroys the vessel that holds it. An attitude of self- importance will get you knocked down, but you will have the opportunity to get back up again.

Having said all of that, our story begins. On a particular Sunday morning, I had prepared a sermon that I just knew would be one of the best I had ever preached. As the service began that morning, I could sense the Lord's presence, the worship was on fire, and as I went to the pulpit, the sense of anointing was almost physical. My topic had to do with prayer and how the power of God was released through our prayers. I can remember at one point in the message when I actually thought, "Yes! I'm nailing this. This is great!" I knew that this was going to end great. Man, I felt good about my own preaching that Sunday.

As I came to the end of my message, I put forth an altar call for prayer warriors. I invited all who wanted to be a part of the power release of God to run to the altar and together we would change our city. I turned and dropped to my knees in front of a chair on the platform and began to call out to God, just knowing this was a life-changing day. Well, I was right, the day was life changing for me but not as I had expected it to be. Kneeling there on the platform praying I noticed that the entire sanctuary was in silence with the exception of my prayer. I glanced over my shoulder to peek at the scene and saw the last of the congregation filing out of the sanctuary in total silence. My heart dropped like a stone to the floor. I couldn't believe this hard hearted bunch.

Saddened I rose to my feet and faced the sanctuary and saw my, son age 14, and his friend still sitting in a pew. At least someone got it. My son and I met at the altar area, and he threw his arms around my neck and hugged me very hard. It was a moment of pure encouragement for me, until he said in my ear, "Dad, the whole back of your pants are ripped out." In a panic I reached both hands to the rear and confirmed his words. I had answered the question "boxers or briefs?" right there on the platform in front of everyone. My next thought was, "How is it possible to be so anointed and so exposed all at the same time?" I began to have a theological crisis about that. Can you be exposed and anointed all at once? And I wondered just how did my suit pants get ripped? These were not some tight fitting jeans, but a decent, if somewhat baggy, suit that I was wearing. It probably wasn't the Lord, but he didn't let me find out until it was way too late. How could He do that to me? My mind and emotions were as torn as my pants.

It wasn't until just after lunch at home that I remembered that I had to go back and preach to those same people at 6:00 o'clock. I began immediately to pen my resignation. I must admit that it sounded funny as I contemplated it. I hereby resign as pastor due to preaching with my trousers ripped from stem to stern. No, that wouldn't do it. So I began to pray, which reminded me of my sermon, and that was difficult.

6:00 o'clock came and I went through the service as if nothing had happened. Exactly no one in the congregation mentioned the morning exhibition. Humbled does not describe how I felt that night. Humiliated is more accurate. The glory hadn't departed from me, but my arrogant attitude sure got dumped. God continued to anoint me, and I continued on in the ministry. But I have to say, I had changed a bit as a result of that embarrassing day.

We know that God is a jealous God for He tells us so Himself in the Scriptures. He doesn't share His glory even with us. So what did happen that day? My best guess at this time is that for some reason either I had just missed something when I got dressed that morning, or God was making a point. Either way that little fall did wonders for my attitude. When God gets involved in our lives in a fashion that adds to our humility it is a form of grace, a grace that helps us lay down something before it becomes deadly, a grace that keeps us from going over the proverbial cliff. So embrace the humility. It's one of the ways God's grace helps us to grow. May you grow tall in the grace of God. And always check your pants before you put them on.

# CHAPTER 35

## CLOSE ENCOUNTERS OF THE FURRY KIND

Out on the back of our five acres I have a woodshed that has five bays with each bay being roughly 12 feet deep and 8 feet wide. When there is wood in this shed it tends to attract pack rats. They are intensely filthy animals and are very hard to get rid of. I try to monitor this shed when I have wood in it to deal with these large rodents before we have too big of a problem and have to discard wood that we planned on using. I went out one afternoon to check and see if any had taken up residence in my woodshed. The first bay of the shed was completely full of firewood, and the one next to it had only one full tier in the back of it. As I walked into the second bay, attempting to spot any unwanted residents in the first bay, I made my way toward the back peering closely at the full shed and stopping just short of the one tier in the back, of the second bay. A small movement caught my eye at the top of the one tier, and I turned to find my nose about four feet from the nose of a very disturbed bobcat. I dare say that neither one of us was happy, but being the more humble of the two of us, I backed carefully out of the shed and let him have it. I guess pack rats attract more attention than I realized.

There are a lot of things in our lives that bear watching lest some social/religious pack rat of habit or feeling take up residence in our stockpile that represents our future hopes and dreams. There are multitudes of people who have dug into their dreams and preparation for their future, only to find some rodent of wreckage has taken up residence, and much of what they had counted on lays in ruin. A simple taking stock on a regular basis can prevent such loss. It's easy to just ignore bad habits and let them set up a permanent nest in the places in our lives that seem to be hidden to most.  Our attitudes, emotions and way of thinking can get infested with critters that foul the wood- sheds of our lives and can leave deposits of odor and other unwanted residue that ruin what we had hoped and planned for.  This can cost us in broken relationships, lost opportunities, and squandered goods that could all have been preserved through a small amount of regular examination.

On the other hand, these unwanted pests that sneak in and find a place of dwelling in our lives can also attract other unwanted guests, some that can actually be dangerous.  Unattended attitudes, habits, and ways can draw the attention of such things as legal battles that could easily have been avoided.  Or they may attract (two-legged) critters that feed on the pests that we refuse to remove from our lives and that can lead to some serious consequences, all because we were either too busy or too lax to maintain a clean shed for our dreams and hopes.  So be careful what you allow to call home in your woodshed.  It might ruin what you have stored there for the future, and it could attract attention from something that you really don't want to meet face-to-face.

# CHAPTER 36

## THE PROBLEM OF FEAR

I had recently dropped out of Bible College as it was not going too well for me, and I had become engaged to the love of my life and just started a new job to make that wedding happen. I had been hired by the U.S. Navy as a civilian employee at Port Chicago in Concord, California and the orientation had left me a bit nervous. The job was to load hundreds of thousands of tons of explosives (roughly 600,000 tons a week) on ships headed for Vietnam. At the job orientation they had talked about potential for large- scale explosions, military use of force on civilians, and given us a full body x-ray so that in the event of an explosion they might recognize us by our bone fragments.

As I exited the transport on the dock on my first day, I could see literally thousands of pallets of bombs stacked everywhere. The 500-pounders were strapped six to a pallet and the 750-pounders were strapped two to a pallet, and they appeared to be endless. The forklifts were buzzing in and out of boxcars that lined the docks three trains deep, and seeing all of this dramatically raised my anxiety level. And that was obvious to everyone around.

My team leader was an older (older than my 20 years) African-American man whose name was George. He noticed me walking around like I was barefoot on broken glass and came to me telling me that, "Here on the dock, I am Daddy George. Don't you worry none cause Daddy George is gonna take care of you!" He took me by the arm, grabbed a large sledgehammer and led me to a stack of palleted 500-pound bombs and told me that I had nothing to worry about. He then drew the sledge-hammer back for a full swing and aimed that swing at the nose end of the bomb (no detonation device attached) and hit that bomb as hard as he could with that sledge-hammer. As he was drawing the sledge-hammer back for his swing, it was obvious what he was going do. I panicked but my feet would not budge, so I placed my two index fingers into my ears, as if that would help, hunched my shoulders, and shut my eyes as tight as I could and waited to disappear in a massive fireball.

When I realized that no explosion resulted from this barbaric display of machismo, I opened my eyes to see Daddy George roaring with laughter. When he finally gained control of himself, he spoke seriously to me. He told me that my only real problem on this job was fear. Fear will stop you from doing what you need to do and will get in the way of you doing your job with competence, and that is dangerous. The bombs themselves are as safe as they can be made to be. The people that handle them are the unknown in this equation. By the end of the first week, I had become familiar with the presence of danger, and fear faded into a sense of respect for the potential, the potential that was in my hands, and the hands of every worker here on the docks. This potential rested firmly in the control of the hundreds of us laborers who were learning to harness our own feelings in this dangerous and foreign arena that we now called a "job."

Fear is one of the more powerful influencers in the lives of people. It takes our normal good sense captive and substitutes a stream of chaotic emotional surges that lack any form of good reason. The result is a flurry of feelings that override our usual solution-response reasoning, and we are left with decision-less actions that have drastic consequences. It is no wonder that the single most frequently repeated exhortation given to us by God, "Fear not," is in the Bible some 365 times.

Fear is a thief to our intellect and emotions. It becomes a dictator to our lives in ways that are almost always devastating. Fear seeks to eclipse all other realities during the time that it rules. It has no concern for our well-being and even less concern for the well- being of others. And I doubt that it was one of the original emotions of our original parents previous to the fall.

This is not to say that all fear is evil. But that sense of terror that destroys our ability to function as people is an enemy, usually the worst enemy in any circumstances. I think that it was President Franklin Roosevelt that said, "The only thing we have to fear is fear itself." Mastering fear is one of the greatest achievements of any person. Forcing our fears into the background and making them submissive to our good sense is a talent that all of us need to cultivate. Fear is one of the enemy's bigger weapons. Fear of failure. Fear of rejection. Fear of pain or punishment. Fear of loss. The list of phobias that assault us people is a very long one, and it is not the intention of our God that we should serve that list in any way. The Scriptures say that, "Men's hearts will fail them because of fear." Fear is unnatural to the Spirit of God. He is entirely unacquainted with fear, and we are also told in Scripture that fear does not come from God to His saints. One of the things that does come from our Lord is sound reasoning. This is opposed to fear.

So, let every diligence be given to slay fear in our lives that we may live in the soundness that God has prepared for us. Fear not. He will never leave you nor forsake you. Thanks, Daddy George! But there should have been a better way to get there.

# CHAPTER 37

## HAIRLINE FRACTURES

It was the mid 1970s, and I was working as a lumber grader in a small redwood mill in Northern California. Ungraded lumber units were brought to me to sort through and trim to get the best grades possible from each board. The market for clear all-heart redwood overseas was huge, and this was what was wanted where possible from each board. One day there appeared to me to be a very large amount of this much-desired grade of wood in the units I was working through. My boss just happened to stop by my work station late that morning, and I commented to him about the strong run of clear all heart wood. He stepped to the unit I had just graded and began to look through it. He found a problem.

He pulled a board out of the unit and told me to take a close look at it and tell him what I saw. I looked closely and saw nothing. He then pointed out the maze of very tiny hair lines running through the board. I had seen them but thought they were nothing, so I saw nothing. I didn't understand his point, and I said so. In response, he took the board, about 12 feet in length, and stood it on end, letting it drop flat on the cement slab. When the board struck the cement, it shattered into several pieces. I could not believe my eyes. I picked up a piece and examined it. It was clear all-heart, without a natural flaw. So I asked, "What was the deal with this?" Then he explained it to me.

It seems as though on occasion when very large redwood trees are felled by loggers, if they hit the ground too hard, the result is all of these hairline fractures that render the log virtually useless for anything but chips or firewood. The log is intact, but when it is milled into lumber, the boards are subject to shattering if struck

110

hard or put under pressure. If they are milled very thin, they will just fall apart. It all looks good, but in reality it is a waste. I had to go through all of the previously graded lumber and discard all of the fractured boards, and there was a lot of them. My production for that day was very low, but my education had been ratcheted up a notch, a fair trade-off for me for that day.

From time to time, we will come across people in church or in association with church who appear to be the real deal. They look like a high-grade believer that is much sought after, and they can make their way into important places in the lives of people, such as marriage and in the structure of the church. They have the talk, and they seem to be a solution for a need in the Body of Christ. But at some time or other, they have fallen hard and are full of hairline fractures. So when pressure comes or they are slapped with obstacles, rejection, or abuse, they suddenly shatter into pieces unexpectedly, and it can leave a lot of pain and problems behind for someone else to clean up. Hairline fractures emotionally, relationally, or in any number of other ways are extremely difficult to see because while they are there, they look like nothing at all if you haven't seen what happens when the pressure strikes. These wounded loved ones of the Lord take their sense of strength and worth from recognition or position and not from the indwelling of the Lord and His Word. I doubt that many of them are trying to do or be anything hurtful, but the fractures have destroyed their resilience and strength, and eventually a problem will ensue.

Unlike redwood, these people are not a useless waste, but they are candidates for love, prayer, and ministry, and they can find healing and solidness with help and understanding. In many churches, there is not a means to minister to these people, and so they go through life fractured or shattered, and at least a few of them really want to be whole, but without loving assistance, they tend to fall through the cracks of discipleship in our churches.

Whatever our problems or baggage as Christians, we need to find solutions to it, especially if we want to end up in a close relationship or a leadership role. When someone notices a hairline fracture in our lives, if we are smart, we will seek help with that area, lest we come under too much pressure and the fracture becomes several shattered pieces. The book of Proverbs speaks of the wisdom of counsel and reproof. Being open to these is difficult but usually produces fruit and health in our lives.

If you feel like you need recognition or a position to be something, you just might have a few hairline fractures that need tending. For the sake of others, especially those whom you love, get the help and healing you need. It is a lot easier than putting the shattered pieces back together -- Humpty.

# CHAPTER 38

## A TREE TOO TALL

I had met and become friends with a very outdoor sort of guy in the church. He was intelligent and capable in a lot of ways, and I admired his abilities and enjoyed spending time with him. Among the many things that we did together, we went woodcutting. I learned a great deal from this man about woodcutting, including how to "fell" trees. Until I met him, the only trees I had cut down were a few smaller oaks. He taught me about cutting larger conifers such as pine, fir, and cedar. He helped me get over my apprehension of falling these trees, and he taught me about how to do so in a safe manner.

On one occasion, while all of this was still new to me, we made our way out into the forest searching for dead trees that would make good firewood and were legal to cut. He spotted a nice cedar back off the old logging road we were on and steered his old Chevy pickup out into the vicinity of the tree and stopped, turned off the motor, and prepared to cut down the tree. I looked at the fairly tall dead tree and where he had parked, and I asked him which way he thought the tree would fall. He said it would fall toward the pickup and would be close enough without hitting the pickup that we wouldn't have to carry the wood far to load it. As he prepared his chainsaw I mentioned that it looked pretty close and could hit his pickup, to which he said, "Nah, lots of room."

So I moved back to a spot that was more than safe to watch the show. He had done this more times than I could count, so I would just watch and help when the time came. Sure enough the tree fell exactly where he said it would, with one small hitch. He had miscalculated the length of the tree and the very top struck the right front fender of his pickup, putting a sizable dent in it. I walked over to examine the dent and found large pieces of thick Bondo that were a part of the dent. I pulled one off and asked him about all of the Bondo. He smiled and responded that this wasn't the first time he had miscalculated.

Miscalculations are unintentional mistakes made with forethought. They are things that we have worked out in our minds and have laid plans for, and somewhere in our thinking we got something wrong, and so something goes wrong that could have been avoided. That is the rub; they could have been avoided but now must be faced. They are not a matter of ignorance or inability, just a miscalculation. The Scriptures speak of this where following Jesus is concerned. It was Jesus himself that said, "For which of you, intending to build a tower, does not sit down first and count the cost, whether he has enough to finish it." (Luke 14:28)

Our verse speaks of our intentions or the forethought of what we do. It goes on to mention the counting of the cost, or the plan laid, and then speaks to the calculation, will this work? That seems to be a pattern in a lot of things in life. To skip one of these steps is not a miscalculation; it is neglect and quite unwise. One of the points that Jesus is making is simply that there is a desired outcome, and we normally go through a process to calculate reaching that outcome. If we have misinformation we will have a miscalculation, and the result will be an error that we thought would not be there, and that adds a great deal of frustration to life. Jesus is telling us that we need to do the same process in following Him. Intent, forethought, plan, and reach what we are after.

Miscalculations happen all of the time. We might miscalculate our budget in regards to a purchase and end up owing what we cannot afford. Or we might miscalculate the schedule of a vacation and miss out on something we wanted to do. Or we might miscalculate the terms and time involved in a relationship and end up with hurt feelings or worse. Just about everything in life offers the opportunity for a miscalculation. And the thing is this, once we are committed to our endeavor, we will have no option but to live with the outcome, good or bad. I can still remember my friend's smile. Looking back on that occasion, I think it was an appropriate response. What else was there to do? Smiles may not always be appropriate, but the sense of readjusting yourself to a new situation and facing it is appropriate.

Far too often we fail to calculate or count the cost, as Jesus said, about something we are wanting to do. Of the two motives (want and need) for doing a thing, want is surely the one that most often sets us to doing something and leaves us in a bind because we miscalculated. Miscalculation will bring about a whole new set of circumstances that you simply cannot just dismiss. We find ourselves at times entangled in things we want nothing to do with because we miscalculated on something we wanted, and we now face something we don't want. So the path into many of our problems is one we set for ourselves because we miscalculated. With such being the case, blaming others is a deceptive and bad approach to problems we end up with. It would have been silly for my friend to blame either the tree or his pickup for the dented fender. He had to shoulder it. That was the only way out. Blaming others or things will not relieve us of the responsibility or the necessity of dealing with what has arisen.

The more we seek to shift blame, the more foolish we become. The more we condemn ourselves in these situations, the more bleak things appear. To avoid a burden that is too heavy, accept responsibility, refuse self-condemnation, ignore the negative response of others, and face the new situation with a whole new set of calculations while calling on the Lord. Deal with life as it happens. Do not let it pile up or you will be buried. Don't let unexpected problems dictate to you your state of mind or emotions. Learn to live mentally, emotionally, and spiritually above the unplanned and unwanted problems. Joy and peace are a state of living, not emotions subject to events. Miscalculations will happen, so determine a path through them and get beyond each as it occurs. Do not fall prey to these unexpected traumas, but rule over them with wisdom and perseverance. And you might want to figure things with a little extra wiggle room, just in case you have miscalculated.

# CHAPTER 39

## DAIRY SKIING

When I was a sophomore in high school, I lived in a farming area. There was all manner of farms from hay to cattle. Dairy farms were in abundance, and I knew another kid whose parents owned a dairy farm. I once went to visit this classmate on the farm owned and operated by his family. When I arrived, it happened to be milking time, which occurred twice a day, every day, all the time. When it is milking time, the milking of these cows takes precedence over all other chores. The cows had come into the holding pen that led into the milking barn, and on occasion one of the cows would be difficult to get into the barn. This problem had led my friend to a sport that would never make the Olympics. In fact, he is the only one I have seen do this. Dairy skiing. Let me explain.

In the holding pen for the cows, because they were there twice a day for some time, the ground was literally a soup of cow excrement several inches deep. If you have ever driven anywhere close to a dairy farm, you know the odor of this soupy slop that marks a dairy farm with its own distinct characteristic.

As I watched my friend attempting to get a particular animal into the milk barn, the cow would continually turn at the last minute and trot back into the pen of odorous slop. The young cow herder looked over at me as I stood outside of the fence and the slop and asked if I had ever skied. Well, I never had, and I didn't know what that had to do with his problem. He walked over to me and said, "Watch this." He then took off his rubber boots, (he was not wearing socks) climbed into the mess, and approached the nether end of the animal of tribulation and quickly grabbed the tail, leaning back just a bit, the cow did the rest. She took off to get away from the irritating thing on her tail and as she ran, he skied through the mess creating a slow moving wake as he was dragged around barefoot in the - mess. He hollered and laughed, and the cow ran faster, and I waited for him to fall, which he never did. He eventually let go, slowed to a stop, and walked back to where I watched in bewildered amazement and asked if I wanted to give it a go. Not on your life. And I never went back to his farm. I had a choice; he really didn't. That makes a difference in a lot of things in life.

There are seasons when we find ourselves by necessity wading in a sloppy mess that only necessity could get us into. We don't want to be there yet there is no way out, and we have to learn how to survive, or even thrive, in the odorous soup we find ourselves in. As crazy as it was, dairy skiing was that young fellow's way of doing more than just surviving the circumstances he was in until he would reach an age to make his own decision about dairy farming. I admire his ingenuity and sense of adventure, but no way would I by choice join him in that pen of manure. I have felt the same way at times about the lives of others. They somehow were surviving and even thriving, but don't ask me to volunteer to join them. I have enough such holding pens in my own in my life. I don't need someone else's.

There seems to be something strange about a person laughing and having fun in manure that is well over ankle deep. Yet his approach to what he was stuck with was a lesson in life that I will not, cannot forget. When life locks you into a pen of manure, just take up skiing in it. Live life as fully as your imagination will allow you to. Find fun and adventure where it seems like there is none. Who knows just who may be watching you and what they are going through, and your twisted sense of adventure may be what they need to start living again, even though they are knee deep in life's

118

castings.  Laughter should not be dependent upon circumstances. It should be free to roam every part of life and spread its own sweet perfume over the odor of manure that has been left behind for you to wade in.

I have learned to admire people who can find life and joy where most would find depression and sorrow.  It is a quality that carries with it a sense of spiritual power unlike most others.  It can lift off weight and give way to a sense of freedom, even in a pen of cow manure.  So refuse to live as a prisoner of smelly things and situations, and let those around you stand in awe, even if you are the only one in history to take that approach in your situation.  Kick off the boots and wade in, have fun, and eventually things will change and you will have a testimony few others have heard.

# CHAPTER 40

## EVERYONE MATTERS TO GOD

I had graduated from high school and went off to Bible College as a yet-new believer in Christ. I was filled with excitement, not over the education I would receive but about living in such close quarters with a few hundred other Christians, both students and teachers. I knew very little about the Bible and Christians, but I couldn't wait to experience life with a whole bunch of people who loved Jesus and would love me. I had issues with love, accepting and giving of it both, and I thought that in Bible school I would find that love in abundance and with it a healing for my soul. What I found was something other than what I had expected, and it would leave me with a sour disposition for a long time to come. That would be my fault, but I could not embrace that at the time.

I found that the student body of the school was made up of people much the same as in any setting. I knew I had issues, but I did not expect the other students to have any. I felt a lot of rejection and disapproval and became a bit antagonistic and quarrelsome, some might call it "rebellious." They would be right. For me, friends were as scarce as hen's teeth, and my loneliness and despair came in waves that made it impossible for me to apply myself to my studies, and I was soon in trouble with the school leaders. I was withdrawn and often slept through large parts of the day, not even trying to attend class. I decided to make an attempt at getting some help and called a teacher/advisor and made an appointment to see him in his office.

I arrived outside of the advisor's office a couple of minutes early. The door was open perhaps six inches or so, and I could hear two people talking inside. I peeked through the door and was noticed by another student that was talking to the advisor. The student mentioned to the advisor that I was there, and the response of the advisor sent me into a tunnel that would take me a long time to recover from. I heard him say, "Oh, he doesn't matter. He will never make it here anyway." I quietly left, abandoning my appointment, and set out to break the rules wherever I could, and I got quite adept at it. I certainly got the attention of the faculty and staff and was often called into some office to give account of some rebellious behavior that I was guilty of. I argued, blamed, and even called names. Since I didn't matter anyway, what difference did it make?

It would be a lot of years before I could let even the Lord into this dark cloud that hovered constantly within my soul. It left me unsure if I mattered to God. I certainly did not matter to His people, so did one equal the other? I was fearful that it did. As I spiraled downward academically and emotionally, I stirred a very negative and harsh response from those whom I wanted to be a part of and then blamed them for reacting in the fashion that I programmed them to. If I didn't matter to them, they didn't matter to me. Eventually this episode would began to play a role in my life that would allow me to help some out of similar dark closets of depression and despair. It would, in fact, become something that would be useful in God's Kingdom and in the ministry. But the road to that was long and difficult and not of my choosing. Jesus, however, had a plan for healing that would reach beyond my own pain and touch a number of others. I had not signed up for this, but it is now something I would not turn down, and look forward to working with others on, because everyone matters to our Lord.

It is easy as Christians to bypass those who appear to be less than desirable. It is, in fact, something that we intentionally practice.

God, however, like with the woman at the well, or the Gergesene Demoniac, or the tax collector Levi, is concerned over and in love with these rejects of our society to the point of making them key players in His incredible work of redemption. They matter. Jesus is very intentional about reaching out to them, not because they appear to offer a key to ministry, but because they are so much in need of ministry that they become key. I feel like I fit into that usually overlooked and frequently avoided group of misfits that on the surface are nothing but failure and trouble but are made to be keys, because to Jesus, everyone matters.

We all know and run into these people from time to time, and few of us have any real regard for them. We pass them as quickly as we can, doing our best to not make eye contact, and we use them as profound bad examples to make our points with others. I am amazed at how much God can change these people, us people. The worse we are, the greater the magnitude of God's grace and glory, and the more visible His Kingdom becomes. For the most part, the powerful changes and influences in Scripture come through this group of people. Much like Jesus, they are rejected as trouble and passed by as quickly as possible. But they still matter.

No amount of rejection, abuse, or neglect will tarnish the appeal of these folks in the eyes of Jesus. The more broken they are, the more insistent Jesus becomes about His care for them. Their need for Him allows Him to do things with them that most others cannot even imagine being possible. They are the miracles of human nature that proclaim God's greatest ability, to love and make a difference, because everyone matters to Him.

May we learn that no person is unimportant because of their past or current failures. They are important because of the contrast those failures will permit after Jesus has touched their lives. Perhaps we can look a little deeper at these social rejects and see the target that they are of God's Spirit and plan. And just maybe, we can become part of that as we let them matter to us because everyone matters to Jesus.

# CHAPTER 41

## LEARNING WHAT YOU PREACH

Over the years, I have preached or taught from the Word of God thousands of times. And I would guess that the most frequent topic over the years has been the love of God for us. I never tire of this subject, though I think that many hope that His love negates their responsibility to Him, and it doesn't work like that. I was involved with ministry for 16 years, which included pastoring three churches and some staff ministry before I began to accept God's great love for me. Most of what I remember from growing up was a lot of hostility that made me feel unwanted and unloved. I don't remember to this day ever being hugged and told "I love you" as I grew up. So when I would preach about the love of God, I was sure it applied freely to everyone, except me. Somehow I felt the need to earn God's love. Not His salvation; I knew I was saved, but I was unsure about His love until something very frightening happened.

My wife of some 17 years had been experiencing a great deal of pain in her upper abdomen that knifed through to her back. We did not have any medical insurance and very little money, so we were slow about going to a doctor to have her checked out. The pain became so severe that we went to the hospital emergency room, and before too long she was admitted with gallbladder problems. This was something more than the usual gallstones, but nobody could tell us just what it was. She was not a candidate for the simple laparoscopic surgery where they used a laser to remove the gallbladder without having to make any large incisions. She lay in the hospital bed for four days in intense pain while the doctors worked out a plan. They decided they would need to do it the old fashioned way, open her abdomen and go in and remove the gallbladder, and have a look to see what else was going on.

They took her into the operating room, telling me it would probably be a couple of hours, so after over three hours I was worried. When the surgeon finally came out to talk with me, he explained that they had discovered a congenital birth defect in the passageway from the stomach to the gallbladder that required some extensive reconstructive surgery, as well as removing the gallbladder. They emphasized that this had turned into a very serious surgery and that she would be in intensive care for at least a few days. When I was allowed in to see her, I was shocked by all of the tubes and machines and her unconscious state. The doctor told me then that if she survived through that first night she would have a 50/50 chance of recovery. I was terrified.

I spent that night in a straight-backed chair by her bed and didn't sleep at all. I kept looking at her and pleading with God to spare her. I needed her. I loved her and I just could not face losing her. Sometime during the middle of the night as I stared at my wife through tears, I heard that quiet but certain voice of the Holy Spirit begin to speak to me about love. He told me that as much as I loved her, He loved her far more. Then He told me that the love I felt for her was small compared to His love for me. I began to weep, and as my wife lay there struggling to recover, I began my own struggle to recover from a lifetime of pain and fear. Apparently, we both had birth defects. We spent that night and a few more in that intensive care unit with both of us in recovery, hers was physical while mine was emotional and spiritual. That was the point where I began to accept His love. It was always there, but I could not embrace it. I have come to where I no longer doubt His love, but I still have a hard time when I look at myself in the mirror knowing what I know about me. Yet at every juncture in this journey in Jesus, He reaffirms His love for me and reminds me that if I can love, being flawed, how much more is He able to love being perfect in every way.

The Lord still reprimands me when I need it, and I can now rejoice in that. He is my Father, and Fathers always work to steer their children on the best course possible for them. When I stumble, I find it much easier to go to my true Father and lay out before Him my failures, and He is faithful to forgive me and help me back to my feet, and with a hug sends me back out to play. He loves Me. I am just sorry that it took my wife going through such a difficult episode for me to come to terms with something that I spoke of all the time to others but felt I somehow didn't qualify for myself. Yep! He loves me.

The love of God is beyond mankind's combined ability to grasp or explain. We are still finding depths in that vast ocean of grace that we will never be able to plumb. His love for me makes me want more than ever to live in a fashion that is pleasing to Him. Not for the sake of rules, though they do exist, but because I am compelled by love to want to be the reason He smiles. His favor and rejoicing over me is what I want. It is what I am finding continually.

My wife recovered from her surgery a long time ago, and she has never been bothered with that problem again since. I've mostly recovered from my surgery too, and while I know that He loves me and that I love Him, I suspect that the magnitude of His love is yet more than I know. But given time, eternity actually, I think I will get to know it pretty well.

# CHAPTER 42

## PEOPLE SKILLS

While pastoring my second church, I worked for a few years in a hardware store, and for the last three years working there I managed the store. One of the employees that worked under me was a jovial fellow with a quick wit and an easygoing manner. On one occasion, a recently divorced lady approached him in the store, carrying one of the toilet seats from the plumbing fixture isle and asked him, "Do you think I could put this on myself?" His response was a quick, "You probably could but I think you would look funny in it." I turned away to laugh, but the customer missed the point of his pun entirely, which made it all the funnier to me.

On another occasion a woman who had purchased the cheapest shovel we had, saying that she would only use it one time so quality did not matter, came back with the shovel and was a bit peeved. "This thing is worthless," she said to Bill (not his real name). Then she proceeded to blame him for selling her this cheap shovel. Bill sought to remind her that he had told her that when she was purchasing the shovel, she had said it did not matter. That just made her mad. After her next tirade, Bill stopped, stood up straight, and said, "Lady, you can just jump back on your broom and fly out of here." He then walked away from her leaving me to finish with her.

Dealing with people is something that we all must do for most of our lives. How we handle people will affect our lives in many ways. It will also become the trail of blessing or sorrow that we leave in our wake. You will be remembered by how you handle the tough ones, so learning something about relationship building is important in life.

My personal clinical profile states that I am totally not a people person and that it is best for people to stay out of my reach when they speak with me. I could see the trail of tears as I grew into adulthood but had a hard time turning that around as relating to people was just not natural to me. I once said from the pulpit that, "I love the ministry. It's all of you people I can't stand." Not one of my better moments.

I found it necessary to take extended trips alone into the mountains to replenish my relational energy. I truly wanted to do better with people, but I had to work at it. I have no regrets for the labor that I have invested in learning how to walk with my fellow human beings. In fact, I have found a great deal of rewards and memories that will bless me till I pass from this world. If I could give all who read this the ability to live well among the rest of the planet, I would. Not having that ability, I encourage those who are born as my descendants, to care about others and learn to build relationships. It is a labor well worth doing. It is also the only truly meaningful thing that you will leave behind in the form of memories.

As a result of my struggles with connecting with people, I enrolled in a School of Behavioral Studies dealing with Temperament Theory and eventually obtained a Pastoral Counselors License to help me interact with others. I learned a great deal about people in general, and while I later laid down my counseling license, I continued to use what I had learned about myself and others to give my relationships the best chance for success that I could. Relationship is the only true reality. Ownership is far too selfish and subjective to be considered a reality. It is more of an unstable condition that can cripple a person's relational life. There are many who approach relationships from the perspective of ownership, and most of the time that results in disappointment and heartache. You do not and can never own a loved one. You can only live within or sometimes outside of the boundaries of that relationship. So learning to relate is one of the most critical and rewarding skills that a person can obtain.

Learn to separate your ownership quotient from your relationship goals. A relationship is stewarded and not owned. It is in constant need of tending and cannot be stored or spent. It is something that is lived with increase or decrease but never really controlled or possessed. It takes the developing of a lot of personal interactive energy and patience if it is to be rewarding. It is more work than we would generally like it to be, but it holds the potential for the greatest reward and satisfaction.

And finally here, learn to see people within the context of relationship, not just behavior. Behavior affects relationship but relationship is intended to be much more than behavior. It is the intersection of multiple behaviors, and one must heed the traffic signals sent out from those within range of the intersection. Key concepts here include maintaining a posture that holds and gives dignity, along with the practice of listening far more than you speak. The welfare of the other(s) in the relationship tends to become your own. So see to it that everything possible is done to sustain the other, knowing that the relationship will tend to reflect the energy you spend on it.

# CHAPTER 43

## REMOVING REPROACH

A few years before I retired from pastoring, I was asked to visit the parents of some young adults in my church. The parents were of the Catholic faith, but we all had a good relationship, so I was happy to go and pray for the mother who was suffering from a serious illness. After a time of prayer and visiting, the father of the family shared a story with me, something that had just happened in the middle of the night before I came over.

He told of hearing noise in his backyard that was separated from an alley by a six-foot- high solid wooden fence. When he went out to investigate, he found a man tossing rounds of firewood over the fence from his yard into a pickup parked in the alley. Cutting firewood was how my friend made his living, so this was real money to him. As he went out into the yard, he called to the man who was taking the firewood and told him to climb into the back of the pickup to stack the wood, and he would hand the wood across the fence to him. With a look of shock, the would-be thief did as he was told, and together they loaded the pickup with as much wood as it would hold. My Catholic friend then gave the man his phone number and told him to call in the next couple of days, and he would take him out and show him where to cut wood and how. The man agreed, and a couple days later the pair were in the woods, the victim of the attempted robbery now the mentor and the would-be thief now the beneficiary of the older man's knowledge and expertise.

I have often marveled at this tale of helping a would be thief by the one who was the target of the theft, and the building of a friendship out of what could have been devastation to both. The thing that amazed me was that my friend seemed to think that this was the only way to handle such a situation, not once considering involving the police. That is grace and redemption on a grand scale.

So often when we are being wronged, our hearts and minds turn to justice and vengeance when a bit of grace will provide a far better outcome. Instead of being so concerned about being wronged, perhaps we should be more concerned about alleviating the need that sends another into desperate and devious measures.

All too often we take the command of the Lord to "love one another" as implying that it is something we do when all is okay, when it might actually be a love response to a wrong that has been initiated by another that would hurt us in some way.

In taking this path, my friend eliminated the theft, thus eliminating the guilt, while filling a desperate need at the same time. When he went the second mile of taking on the challenge of mentoring the man who would rob him, He displayed a Christ-like character that is rare, even among the closer followers of Jesus.

It just goes to show you that when something wrong is taking place, the right response has the power to free the captive and empower him as well. Sounds so much like Jesus. And my friend just acted as if that was the normal thing to do. His humility added a touch of grace that still leaves me in awe. Who would guess that obeying the difficult instructions of the Lord could be so liberating and in the end, build a relationship that everyone benefits from.

We often feel that we have the right to be offended when we have been wronged, but not so. Offending situations are not a right but an opportunity to give life to the offender. There are no such pregnant situations as when one is wronged and chooses a path of grace over the attitude of hostility. Who knows what will come forth from such times and circumstances. Modeling what Jesus taught is a lot harder than prevailing upon His grace for our own needs. Accepting grace is a beginning; dispensing it is the ideal. Everything stored in a vessel needs to be poured out sometime, usually when it is most needed. So it should be with grace in us, stored for a time when someone else needs it.

# CHAPTER 44

## BREAKING TRAIL

We were about five years into our third pastorate when we found out that one of our daughters, still single, was pregnant. As I talked on the phone with a friend about this, telling him that I planned on leaving the ministry, his tone of voice changed, and he became mildly upset. I will never forget what he said to me, especially since I wanted nothing to do with it. He said, "We all know how to quit when things get tough. Why don't you show us how to go through it the right way?" The irritation in his voice along with the words he spoke left me angry and feeling sorry for myself. What did he know? I was expecting some kind of gentle understanding pity, and instead he said what I really needed to hear. How insensitive is that? I wanted no part of doing this right, only the Spirit of the Lord would not allow me to escape those words.

Do it right? When you are wounded and tired and have no desire to do anything right? I knew almost immediately what the Lord was requiring of me, and I also knew that just about everyone would understand if I didn't do it right. And then it became clear that for my own family's sake, I needed to do this the right way. So I set about to take each painful step, one at a time, and help my family and my church to walk through this in a Godly fashion.

We all can find ourselves in an unwanted setting that was not our doing, and yet it is up to us to demonstrate the good in the middle of the struggle. The big temptation, to play on the sense of pity that those around you will offer up in abundance, is one of the most natural things you can do, and it is usually one of the worst things you can do. There is an overabundance of examples of going through a tough time thinking about how you feel, but very few show us how to do it right thinking about what others in the situation need from you.  Do it right.  Break trail for those who will follow this way.

I have lived in snow country for a number of years now, and if you have ever walked in snow that is even knee deep, breaking trail or going ahead of the others, you know this is hard and can be dangerous.  The trail breaker not only creates a path for others, but he also is the first one to encounter the hidden difficulties that lay under the snow.  Yet it is imperative that someone do this and prepare a path for the rest.  Jesus in the Garden of Gethsemane had to decide whether or not to do redemption right.  It was an agonizing decision, and He got no help from His closest friends. He was breaking trail for the multitudes who would be faced with the decision to obey God or take the path of least resistance, one that would relieve of all of the difficulty but leave nothing for those who still needed to travel the rough road.

Through the years that followed this, I have sat with a number of people and gave them essentially the same advice that I received that day.  I doubt that any of them liked it any more than I did.  In fact, some adamantly refused to break trail for their family and friends and left a testament to the devastation that being self-minded can bring in those situations.  I know of only a couple others who took the advice.  They, after a time, found that their life still had a future as a result.  That is what breaking trail is all about. Keeping a future when the past seems to have stolen it.  Do it right, and you can one day see things right.  Do it the easy way, and the present might be a little easier, but the price will be the future. Living through tough times and situations with the future of others in mind requires a far greater commitment than does living with self-comfort in mind.

Living it right does more than just keep the future open, though. I have found that it will eventually lay the past to a peaceful, even joyful rest. It does a great deal to keep regret from finding lodging in our lives, and it allows us to speak of the past without pain. So do it right when all is wrong. It improves both the future and the past, while giving the present a genuine sense of purpose and hope.

# CHAPTER 45

## A CHILD'S TEA PARTY

My wife had invited some of the ladies of the church over to our home for refreshments and a time of visiting together. Our two oldest daughters (our youngest two children not yet having arrived) were in their bedroom playing house and having a private little tea party of their own. As the ladies sat around our living room visiting, our firstborn came down the hall with a child's teacup of water and offered it to one of the ladies, who graciously accepted the cup. She drank the water, expressed her thanks, and mentioned how cute that was, then gave the cup back to our daughter who turned and went back down the hall. A couple minutes later my daughter returned with another teacup of water and offered it to a different lady who again accepted the cup, commenting on just how cute this was. Again, my daughter returned back down the hall and brought back yet another small cup of water.

As this was going on, my wife watched and enjoyed the attention that our daughter was getting, until she thought, "I wonder where she is getting the water?" Then, in a panic, my wife went down the hall, into the bathroom and, "Oh NO!" Our daughter was dipping the teacups into the toilet. It was the easiest access for her, and then she had been serving this to the ladies in our living room. All so cute. Yet all so wrong. And with the enormous potential for some very unhealthy results in the long run.

Needless to say, our daughter's cute little tea party ended abruptly, and nothing was said to the ladies gathered in our living room. We had concerns that one or more of these ladies could get very sick, so we watched and prayed and saw no ill effects. This all then became our private little secret for a number of years.

136

I have, at times, when coping with some strange beliefs that would enter the church through a well-meaning parishioner, thought of this little tea party. How cute and sincere something can be, yet how much potential for sickness and brokenness in a life. Accepting every little drink of water offered to you may not be such a good idea. The water that my daughter offered up would have been just fine had it not passed through a toilet bowl first. Sometimes that is true with information, even Scripture. Where something comes from can be as important as what it is. All too often Scripture can be offered up by someone whose own spiritual life contains a bacteria similar to what is found in a toilet. The truth is easily contaminated by the vessels that it is dipped out of. Not all who quote Scripture text are telling the truth. In some cases, it may be innocent error or just ignorance. But in many cases it is just contamination by contact and mixing in a cesspool of religious bacteria that bring on a host of spiritual ailments.

The Scriptures tell us to, "Know those who labor among you," not just what they teach or where they serve, but know the vessel. Learn something of the pool that this vessel offers from. I have frequently picked up a glass that I had used earlier, and then left on the counter, to get a drink from. But I always glance inside the glass to be sure it is still clean enough to be safe to drink from. Know those who minister to you the Word of God. Their lives are as telling as what they speak. You want to drink water from the spigot, not the toilet. You may well survive toilet water, but it is never a good source.

The Scripture talks about various "winds of doctrine" that blow through the church on a regular basis. A clean vessel will not pour forth bacteria-laden lessons just because they are popular at the moment. We also know from Scripture that, "A fountain does not bring forth both good and bad water". It will be one or the other.

So check out the fountain before you dip your teacup into it. Once you find a good one, drink often, and hang out around that fountain. Don't be easily moved away from a pure fountain for the promise of a better-flavored water. There is no telling what is being used to flavor the water. Cute and sincere are wonderful; they just are not enough to trust your life to. So I hope you have a lot of fun tea parties but check the source before you tip up your cup.

# CHAPTER 46

## WHY ME?

I had just recently enrolled in Bible College and knew I needed to go to church, so this particular Sunday I chose one of the larger churches in the area in a town just a few miles from the college I was attending. I was just 18 years old and had no connections or relationship with this church. My attendance on this Sunday was just a random choice to me. I entered the church a few minutes before service time, found a center- aisle seat on the right hand side about a third of the way from the back of the sanctuary and sat down. The service soon started. In those days, no one stood on their own to worship. The song leader told you when to sit and when to stand, and most of the time you did not stand until the last song.

We had just been instructed to stand and had just started singing the final hymn when I felt a tap on my shoulder. I turned to find a tall, large man in a sport coat standing directly behind me. I did not know him, but I listened to what he had to say. He pointed out a young man about my own age perhaps five or six rows ahead of me with a seat next to the aisle as was mine. He then told me that the young man he had pointed out was ready to receive Jesus and be saved. He further stated that if I would go up to the young man and ask him if he wanted to receive Jesus he would say yes, and then I could lead him to the altar and to the Lord. My mind immediately asked the silent question, "Why me?" I was a visitor for the first time in this church and knew neither the large man behind me nor the young man he had pointed out. I had no clue as to how things were done in this church or if it was even all right to go to the altar without instructions from the pulpit. So why me?

For some strange reason I felt quite intimidated by the large man who was asking me to do this odd thing. I really did not want to do it. I did ask him, "Why me?" His response was to tell me that the young man was mine and not his. That sounded strange but I could not come up with a good reason to tell him no, so I stepped out and walked, ever so self-consciously to the young man, stopping beside him and tapping him on the shoulder. I asked him if he wanted to receive Jesus as his Savior, honestly expecting him to say no. He immediately became teary of eye and nodded his head yes, so I told him to come with me, and we walked to the altar where we knelt. With just a few words of instruction, I then prayed with him to receive the Lord. We both hugged there on our knees, stood, and walked back to our respective seats. I had not asked him his name or given mine. This all took place in perhaps three minutes or less.

I have never seen either of these two men again since that morning, and I have never said another word to them beyond that brief exchange during the final song of the church service. The question, "Why me?" lingered for a long time after this. Was it because we were about the same age? Or was it because I was the only one who would feel intimidated enough to do this? Was it an appointment made in heaven? And I have long wondered just who the big guy was. I have come to a tentative conclusion that he could well have been an angel. If so, he would be the first of at least three that my earthly life would intersect with.

Throughout our lives we will face situations, both good and bad, where we will be left with the question, "Why me?" And in the majority of these situations that question will not be answered this side of eternity. I have found that God, though clear with his instructions, is not big on explanations about much of anything.

Most of the conclusions we reach concerning this disquieting question will be little more than conjecture. So my point is this, you can expect to have a number of unexplainable things in your life, especially if you serve the Lord. Get used to this, and work at not manufacturing "Why me?" conclusions. Accept what the Lord brings your way and count these times as opportunities for the practice of faith in the long term. Unanswered questions where God is concerned are one of the greatest opportunities to exercise faith that you will ever encounter. Abram was instructed to leave his hometown without any real explanation. That was one of the biggest things that earned him the title of "Father of Faith." He acted without any answer to the, "Why me?" question. Acting with instruction but without understanding is a pure faith circumstance. The more understanding we require, the less faith is relied upon. The less we rely upon faith, the smaller our accomplishments become in the Lord. So, when the "Why me?" question strikes, just lay hold of faith. The answers to all of these questions will make for some awesome moments in heaven when all is revealed and the work that our faith has accomplished is rewarded. Maybe it is about something yet to come, way out there in our future in another place. And besides, "Why not you?"

Made in the USA
Coppell, TX
23 August 2021